THE
CORPSEWOOD
MANOR
MURDERS
IN NORTH GEORGIA

THE
CORPSEWOOD MANOR
MURDERS
IN NORTH GEORGIA

AMY PETULLA

THE
History
PRESS

Published by The History Press
Charleston, SC
www.historypress.net

First published 2016

Manufactured in the United States

ISBN 978.1.46711.900.9

Library of Congress Control Number: 2016936015

CONTENTS

ACKNOWLEDGEMENTS

I want to thank the many people of the Lookout Mountain Judicial Circuit who gave so generously of their time to bring this book to life. From the attorneys and judges and clerk's office staff to law enforcement and probation, the secretarial staff at all those places and the friends and acquaintances of Charles Scudder and Joseph Odom, everyone has been wonderful about sharing their stories and memories, and I cannot thank you enough. Among those to whom I am most indebted are: Bobby Gilliland, who not only spent hours sharing his knowledge but also took me out to Corpsewood twice and shared his personal photos from the crime scene with me; Ralph Van Pelt, who shared photos as well as recollections; Jon Dennis (who, besides being a wonderful storyteller, is also an awesome photographer, as well as an authority on Howard Finster and William Blake); and Cindy Hall, Johnny Bass, Ben Ballenger, Judge and Mrs. Joseph E. Loggins, Jim and Herbert "Buzz" Franklin, McCracken Poston (who shall forevermore be linked in my mind with "the hot dog case"), Gary McConnell, Christopher Townley, Albert and Kim Palmour, Clifton "Skip" Patty, Judge Jon "Bo" Wood, Bryant Henry, David Dunn, E. Don Towns, Kristina Cook Graham, Melanie Le, Ann Patterson, David Whitman, Archibald Farrar, Brad Bonnell, Dustin and Dee Cochran, Kerri Hamilton, Candice Williamson, John Croy, Jordan Poole and the other folks at Paradise Garden, Magus Peter Gilmore, John Levey, Lin Gray, George C. Coker, Gerald Fleming, Alice Daniel Seabolt, Kent Moreno, all those who asked to remain anonymous, the ladies at the Walker County district attorney's office, the staff of the Chattooga County Library and the wonderful ladies in the Chattooga County clerk's office, especially Doris, who had to hand me the West court file so often, even if it meant some piece of office machinery broke down every time she touched it. I am so grateful to the people who read my drafts and made suggestions, including some of those listed above, as well as Penny Watne, Meredith Casto, Hope Holloway, Shelby Abernathy and Rachel Abernathy. Thanks to Gene Espy of the *Summerville News* for allowing me to use the old photos of the attorneys, and a big thank-you to Stephen King for allowing me to use the reference to Castle Rock. A special thank-you to Mark Fults for filling me in in such wonderful detail on the paranormal aspects of the case. And finally, a big posthumous thank-you to the incomparable David "Red" Lomenick for bringing me to this deliciously wild and wonderful circuit in the first place.

Introduction

Chattooga County, Georgia, is known for two things: the blessed Paradise Garden, home of Howard Finster, bicycle repairman and preacher whose 1976 vision led him to become a renowned folk artist and build his World's Folk Art Church in 1982; and the ill-fated Corpsewood Manor, the castle built by hand in the middle of the national forest as home for two party-loving Satanists.

In 1982, the God-fearing folks of Chattooga County slumbered peacefully, secure in the knowledge that their larger-than-life sheriff was keeping troublesome elements under control. Their lives might be occasionally disturbed by the rantings of street preacher Howard Finster or the drunken drag-racing of bored adolescents, but they were confident that their tiny southern town was safe from the evil that regularly befell large, heathen cities like Atlanta and New York. Little did they know what they harbored in their midst. A dark shadow fell over the town that fall, wreaking havoc and turning their world upside-down. Opinions about what brought it differ wildly. Some say it was pure coincidence. Some say it was born of the convergence of small-town prejudices, warped southern values and an uneducated populace poorly served by Georgia's impoverished education system. And some say it was forged by Dr. Charles Scudder, a Loyola professor of pharmacology and assistant director of the Institute for the Study of Mind, Drugs and Behavior, who relocated to the area from Chicago with his housekeeper/companion, Joey Odom, in 1976. Disillusioned with the rat race, they built a castle in the woods by hand, filled it with Satanic symbols and named it Corpsewood after

Above: Paradise Garden, an iconic folk art sanctuary built by Howard Finster with divine guidance, flourishes with the fruit of Howard's dream. *Amy Petulla.*

Left: Since the murders there in 1982, rumors have swirled about a curse at Corpsewood Manor. Today, only a few crumbling structures remain. *Amy Petulla.*

the graveyard of denuded trees that greeted their arrival. Small-town gossips whisper that Charles claimed he invoked a demon to protect their estate, along with their massive English mastiffs, Beelzebub and Arsinath. The pair worshiped sensual pleasure rather than God, reportedly throwing sex parties for out-of-town friends and, rumor has it, the occasional upstanding citizen on the sly. The bacchanalia came to an abrupt and bloody end in December 1982, when Tony West and Avery Brock came calling. The murders made international news and set the stage for court proceedings peopled with a judge who reportedly didn't believe the Constitution applied in his territory, a jury commission that handpicked its personal grand jury, a colorful district attorney who spat tobacco and invective in court and eventually a world-renowned lawyer said to be the inspiration for the *Matlock* television show. Though the case is long over, Corpsewood continues to haunt the area to this day.

Chapter I

THE TOWN

Lying between the cities of Chattanooga, Tennessee, and Rome, Georgia, is the sleepy little town of Trion, Georgia, population around 1,700, located in Chattooga County. While the rest of the country has been growing, expanding and moving on with life, Chattooga County has remained the Land That Time Forgot. Were you to travel in time from the present to 1982, you might well not even realize you had made the trip, other than some wear and tear on the residents. The same probate judge sits on the bench, the court clerk from that time is only now preparing to retire and the same deputies greet you as you come in the courthouse door. Nor is it only the people who have remained unchanged. The scenery on the way there becomes more and more remote, and this tiny rural refuge from progress appears exactly as it did all those years ago. Long stretches of flat, open road with only the trees for a view, a few stores here and there that may have changed names but are otherwise identical to their earlier iterations, the water/sewage treatment plant with its large round vats brewing—all offer the same placid appearance. A "Paradise Garden" marker now points toward the home of nationally known folk artist Howard Finster; years ago, the townspeople were not so anxious to point out the residence of the "loony street preacher." The courthouse still presides over the square, populated in large part by shops that look like they went out of business decades ago. Natural beauty abounds, as do Christian values. The parks and ponds have not been sacrificed to the development gods, and even the old train depot has been preserved, serving as a gathering place for young and old alike. The

Downtown Chattooga County shops. *Amy Petulla.*

Unexpected beauty in downtown Chattooga County. *Jon Dennis.*

one surprise when traversing this secluded province is the amount of art. Beauty created by both God and man thrives here.

As you approach Trion, there is a nearly imperceptible rise on the scarcely populated five-lane highway. There are mountains in the far horizon on both sides, but "Devil's Mountain," as it has come to be known in the days and years since 1982, raises its head alone in the near distance, presaged only by a sudden treeline in the otherwise barren landscape. The locals avoid this ancient ridge looming above. An eerie fog often rises in Trion just as you pass the turnoff to the landmark, perhaps occasioned by the water treatment plant, but sudden temperature drops of ten degrees or more in the space of just a few flat miles are not so easily explained.

The townsfolk are outwardly friendly toward strangers, at least those who do not appear to threaten their way of life. Not many black faces color the landscape, and you wonder how such a town could have been home to a couple of "devil-worshipping" Yankee homosexuals from Chicago. But like many small towns, Trion tolerates eccentrics, if they are *its* eccentrics. This is the area where a local named Zeke used to enjoy handing out his card, which read, "Zeke Woodall, Nudist. I sure do like running naked!" This area was also home to the phenomenon that was Howard Finster. Howard's story goes a long way toward explaining the mindset of this tiny rural region.

Howard Finster is now known nationally for his folk art—his angels, soft drink bottles and Elvis, among other subjects, all covered with writings proclaiming his own particular brand of Christianity. But in Chattooga County, plenty of people will still tell you Howard Finster was the bicycle repairman. The kids called him "Finister." Others called him the local nut, preaching in a church when he could, on the streets or even on the courthouse steps when he couldn't. Odd, yes. But a national figure, a celebrated artist? The townsfolk would have laughed anyone who suggested that out of town.

The year 1976 changed the sixty-year-old evangelist's life. He had begun his first "garden" museum in Trion in the late 1940s. His plan was to display one example of every single thing ever invented. As one might expect, he eventually ran out of space and expanded in the 1960s to a swampy piece of land in a nearby neighborhood known as Pennville. His focus changed from man-made creations to those of God, but he continued with his bike repair work to bring in some income. One day in the fateful year of 1976, he was doing a patch job on a bike tire when a smudge of white paint on the tip of his finger warped into a face, and the face began talking to him. Its voice echoed in his head, "Paint sacred art. Paint sacred art." Howard responded that he was not a professional artist. The persistent voice simply answered, over and over, "How do you know?" Worn down, Howard took a dollar bill from his pocket, stuck it to a piece of wood and made a painting of George Washington as his first piece of "sacred art." And that was the beginning of Howard Finster's artistic career.

Finster painted his Cadillac in the early '80s with Elvis, angels and moral lessons. At Paradise Garden, it is dusty now, as then. *Amy Petulla.*

Howard Finster's first painting can still be found on a rusting outdoor structure hidden away at the back of Paradise Garden. *Amy Petulla.*

Howard claimed he started having visions at three years old. After the sacred art command, God originally told him to create five thousand paintings, so somewhere on each one of Howard's paintings, you will find its number in the count. Apparently, God amended that figure at some point, as the artist reached the original goal at the end of 1985 but kept frantically creating art right up until the day he died in an effort to, as he put it, "see the last piece put on" the job God had sent him to do. Most estimates put the final tally upward of forty-six thousand. However you calculate it, Howard Finster's body of work was prodigious.

Painting was not his only artistic directive, however. Howard continued to add eclectic (many would say bizarre) elements to his garden. He was literally building Paradise from garbage. You will find on display at Paradise Garden art created from trash, dust-coated old cars covered with portraits of his heroes, a sarcophagus that at one time had a glass window to display the two-hundred-year-old body of a seventeen-year-old girl that had been donated to him after being dug up on a local doctor's property and Howard's own coffin, in which

he wanted his ashes buried, along with one million letters deposited into the coffin by visiting fans. Despite his wishes, Howard's body is buried in Alabama, but his coffin remains.

The crown jewel of the garden, however, is the World's Folk Art Church. God had given Howard another urgent directive in 1982, the same year as the Corpsewood murders, and Howard complied by buying an abandoned church building and turning it into a sanctuary for his work against evil. With only a sixth-grade education and no construction training, he rebuilt the one-story

An unknown body in Howard Finster's Paradise. *Amy Petulla.*

structure into a four-story

Howard Finster's World's Folk Art Church, said by many to resemble a wedding cake. *Amy Petulla.*

wonder with a circular staircase and sixteen sides, from plans he received in this vision from God. It has been repeatedly compared to a wedding cake. One of the first people to call it that was his neighbor, Ethel Olene Dennis, who lived in a short tan house across the street. After completing the chapel, he asked her what she thought about it. She responded, "Well, Howard, I think it looks like a wedding cake," to which he responded, "Well, I think your house looks like a peanut butter sandwich!"

The artist's fame exploded when he did album covers for both the Talking Heads and REM in the 1980s. He did not, however, let fame change him and continued to chat with anyone and everyone who came to visit, often inviting them to camp out in his yard. To Howard, the rich, famous and powerful were no different than the folks who lived down the street. When *Time* magazine wanted to commission him to paint a cover, he told it that its magazine was small, but he would do it to help it out because "I am here to do for others." He appreciated the fame for the sole fact that it helped spread his message to repent. As Howard put it in an interview with Kristine Mckenna in the *LA Times* on October 23, 1988: "Talking Heads offered me $3,000 to make a picture for 'em and I put 26 wholesome verses that the world needs to hear in that cover. And that rock 'n' roll bunch took my 26 verses and in 2½ months they'd covered the world with 'em. They reached more people for me than 40 years of pastoring churches!" He spent the money on more art supplies and the garden to further share his Bible verses, as well as sharing very generously with his neighbors. Having come of age during the Depression, he had a parsimonious attitude toward money. He certainly didn't spend it on himself and his wife, Pauline, who, according to neighbor and local attorney Jon Dennis, had been heard to complain that her husband was so cheap, he wouldn't let her buy a clean pair of drawers. He was, however, always willing to share his wealth and life with those who needed it. Howard Finster at last completed his God-given mission on October 22, 2001, when he left this world behind for greater things. But while the townspeople are proud to have given birth to such a phenomenon, like Jesus, he is still thought of in his hometown as "the bicycle repairman made good" rather than the prodigy seen by the rest of the world.

Howard saw the world differently from most people. He believed, in a way some have described as child-like, that this world was populated by evil and was very clear that he had encountered that evil himself in his life in Chattooga County. Perhaps he did, in a form more tangible than most people can imagine.

For Chattooga County, Georgia, and its surrounds, a tiny remote area of the state, in a very short time span would host four of the most horrific crimes this country had ever seen, crimes that were even more appalling because they were planned and executed by the young or seemingly vulnerable. In the fall of 1982, teenager Judith Neelley and her Trion-born husband, Alvin, who had up until then been run-of-the-mill thugs and thieves, would kidnap thirteen-year-old Lisa Ann Millican from a mall in nearby Rome, Georgia; rape her for days; inject her with Drano;

Janice Chatman's body was so badly decomposed when found that her head had separated from her body. *LMJC District Attorney's Neelley file.*

shoot her; and push her off a cliff.* Thereafter in Chattooga County, they would rape and brutally murder intellectually challenged Janice Chatman and attempt to murder her boyfriend, John Hancock, and leave him for dead. Later, Judith would manage to kill someone miles away while in prison via a "suicide pact" where only the other woman died. She would become the youngest woman ever sentenced to death in the United States after it was established that she was the driving force behind the murderous pair. This area would also see the hellish landscape at Tri-State Crematory, where young Ray Brent Marsh would eventually be charged with 787 criminal counts for abandoning more than three hundred bodies among the grounds to putrefy and rot rather than cremating them. And around the same time, 400-pound schizophrenic Hayward Bissell, who despite his mental illness had

---

* A woman referred to as "M" in order to protect her identity told the author that the Neelleys had tried to lure her into their car earlier that same day at Riverbend Mall. The friends who arrived to pick her up just then without a doubt saved her from a horrible fate. She was quite clear that it was the young woman, not her much older husband, who was in charge.

Right: Judy's October 15, 1983 letter to Alvin declaring her love, claiming full responsibility and stating Lisa was better off dead than in the Youth Development Center. *LMJC District Attorney's Neelley file.*

Below: Bissell killed and dismembered his girlfriend in the gravel lot adjacent to Victory Fuels. *Amy Petulla.*

never before been charged with a violent crime, would shock the world when, in a Trion convenience store parking lot, he brutally butchered his 105-pound girlfriend, Patricia Booher, cutting off her left hand and right leg and tossing them in the car floor, pushing her eyes so far into their sockets that they were originally believed to have been gouged out and then cutting out her heart. Following that, he calmly buttoned her shirt back up, reattached her seat belt and drove on to Alabama to continue his crime spree. When being interviewed by the police, he casually pulled her esophagus out of his pocket and started chewing on it. What concoction bubbled up in this rustic province all those years ago that brought multiple horrific murders in its wake? What conflict left behind such ghastly fallout? The most astonishing and notorious crimes in this provincial community, however, executed by seventeen-year-old Kenneth Avery Brock and his cohort, Tony West, were the Corpsewood Manor murders in North Georgia.

The story starts in 1976. That year, Dr. Charles Scudder, a Wisconsin-born pharmacology professor who had lived for decades with his cook, housekeeper and companion Joseph Odom in a Chicago mansion, sloughed off the bonds of society and relocated with Joey to a remote mountain section of Trion known as Taylor's Ridge, where they were free to indulge in the hedonistic lifestyle dictated by Scudder's recently adopted Church of Satan (CoS) ideology.

Chapter 2

THE VICTIMS

Like the enigmatic Dr. Drosselmeier in *The Nutcracker*, thousands of people who never had the opportunity to meet him have vastly different opinions of Dr. Charles Scudder. Was he the slightly eccentric neighbor next door? The beloved, affable uncle handing out psychedelic treats? Or was he in actuality a much more sinister persona, one battling powerful demons of his own creation? The conflict between conception and reality has led to a hotly contested debate—who was this well-spoken middle-aged man really, and how did he develop into this mysterious amalgamation?

Those who met him almost universally agree: Charles was cultured, brilliant, polished, soft-spoken but confident, with impeccable manners—in a word, urbane. Few photographs of the man during his life exist, but in his death photos, he bore a striking resemblance to the actor who played the father of a certain sparkly vampire clan: blond, well built, good looking, appearing much younger than his fifty-six years. Charles had an easy smile and charming manner, and while very powerful according to his own letters, he was slight in form, only five feet, six inches. He was *not* the stereotypical "devil worshipper" as conjured up by the imagination.

Charles Lee Scudder came into this world in Milwaukee County, Wisconsin, on October 6, 1926, the day Babe Ruth hit his historic record-breaking three home runs in a World Series game against the Cardinals. He was born to Captain Charles Morrison Scudder, a hydraulic and mechanical engineer, and his wife, Eleanor Lee Scudder. He had an older sister, Janet. Both parents had been to college, which was highly unusual back then, and their neighbors on Seventieth Street were likewise highly educated. Charles Morrison Scudder had the highest income on the street.

According to his résumé, Charles studied zoology and languages at the University of Wisconsin. At the age of nineteen, shortly after his father's death, he met and married Helen Kilbourne Hayslette, a twenty-one-year-old co-ed at Oberlin College. Hayslette was not afraid to speak her mind. While a student at Stanford in 1947, she wrote a letter to *Time* magazine disagreeing with the magazine's assertion that no place in the United States had worse public transportation than Chicago by pointing out that San Francisco was in the United States. The marriage did not last long and produced no children. Charles got his master's in 1949 and married Bourtai Bunting, daughter of internationally acclaimed British poet Basil Bunting. Bourtai was an activist back then and remains so to the present day, speaking out and engaging in acts of civil disobedience throughout her life, including actively protesting against the death penalty, regardless of her former employment as an assistant attorney general in the state of Washington. (Although Scudder reportedly told Trion locals that she had died and implied the same in his article for *Mother Earth News*, as of this writing, she is still alive and quite active. She remarried in 1968.) On his résumé, Scudder lists his occupation from 1950 to 1959 as "Independent Farming" in Wisconsin, where he and Bourtai had four children: Saul, Fenris Sorrow, Gideon and Ahab. Ahab died young, according to most reports at the age of seventeen while in his senior year at Carson High School in California. The yearbook contains no memorial page, however, to give a clue about what tragedy befell the youth. Saul and Fenris went on to professional occupations. Gideon, imbued with unnatural luck, won the scratch-off lottery big—twice.

The marriage soured, and in the late 1950s, Charles moved to Chicago. He had an art piece called *Mechanoid II* in a Chicago Artists Exhibition sponsored by the Chicago Arts Institute in 1957, and in 1959, he began teaching biology at the University of Illinois. He enrolled in graduate school at the Stritch Medical School of Loyola University in 1961. Contrary to what many people believe, Scudder was not a medical doctor, but he did acquire his PhD in pharmacology in 1964. This degree allowed him employment much more suited to his burgeoning identity of societal rebel. An associate professorship of pharmacology at the medical school's Department of Pharmacology & Experimental Therapeutics followed, along with the assistant directorship of Stritch's Institute for the Study of Mind, Drugs and Behavior. In that position, the unorthodox professor did government-funded experiments with psychoactive drugs, believed to include the hallucinogenic LSD.

Shortly after moving to Chicago, Charles met Joey Odom. Born Joseph David Terrence Odom on March 27, 1938, in Cook County, Illinois, Joey's life had had far less privilege than Charles's. His father, Connie, born in Georgia, had only a second-grade education and listed his occupation as "hotel linen boy." Working a fifty-two-week year earned him only $853, less than a quarter of what Charles's father made. His mother, Mary, had a fourth-grade education and did housework for others when she could get work, but that did not bring in much. The family had moved shortly before Joey's birth from the Deep South to Chicago, where it was easier to raise the children Catholic. Besides his parents and sisters, his unemployed uncle Peter Condella also lived with them for a lengthy period. Living conditions were cramped. Joey dropped out of school in the fifth grade. Lacking an education and substantial skills, it is not surprising that he got into trouble with the law at some point and was incarcerated. It has been said that he learned to cook while in jail. Not a lot is known about Joey Odom, but one thing everyone agrees on is that the man could cook. As Charles put it in his March–April 1981 *Mother Earth News* article, Joey had "a talent for whipping up meals fit for a king!" His preference was to cook the old-fashioned way, with iron skillets and platters. He eschewed modern-day conveniences and admitted that, if it were up to him, he would simply cook on a wood stove without any electricity. Joey's simplicity was one of the things Scudder loved best about him.

Odom moved into Charlie's West Side Chicago mansion on West Adams Street and served as housekeeper, cook, errand boy and companion. In an article he published in *Mother Earth News* in 1981, Charles implied that Joey helped raise his children, but that may have been a stretch; according to the *Madison Wisconsin State Journal*,

Charles Scudder. State v. Tony West *exhibit file, Chattooga County Court.*

Charles's ex-wife, Bourtai, checked with the office of public welfare to try to recover child support from him on two of their children in 1967, though those efforts, according to the journal, were "stopped cold." It is possible that two of their children may have lived with Scudder and Joey for some period of time, though by the time they moved to Georgia, Charles's children were grown. It is undisputed that whatever the relationship was between himself and his children in their formative years, they became estranged from him in later years. Years before he left Chicago, he would attempt to disinherit his children completely in his will, in favor of Joey.

Several sources have noted that Joey was somewhat feminine. However, Charles told at least one of his correspondents that he himself had taken a personality inventory that revealed that he was 80 percent feminine. None of his close friends expressed that opinion, however.

Charles was not your typical professor. At one point, he dyed his normally dark hair purple. In his later years, he would dye it blond. For a while, he kept a pet monkey. He had a pink gargoyle fountain that squirted water from its mouth at the Chicago mansion; he would later take it with him to Georgia and give it a place of honor above the entrance to his home there. But in these days long before marriage equality, he kept his changing sexual preferences in the closet. No one at Stritch appeared to realize that he was anything other than straight. Those who knew about Joey thought he was simply the housekeeper or cook. If anyone was aware that Charles's religious beliefs were unconventional, they never came forward to say so. And certainly, no one seemed to think there was a possibility that he may have been personally enjoying the fruits of his labor with psychedelic drugs.

Charles became more and more disillusioned with the rat race. He complained about his students becoming more uncontrollable and less interested in developing their minds than their supercilious attitudes. He was fed up with the backstabbing and brown-nosing inherent in the hallowed halls of higher education. His neighborhood was dilapidating around him, drawing down property values for a home that was simultaneously sucking up more and more money.

Charles and Joey's ties with Chicago and the mansion were further torn as they lost their remaining parents during their residency there. Joey's mother passed away in December 1966. Less than six months later, in a cruel mirror of the future, his father was viciously attacked by a mugger and died from complications associated with his injuries a few months later. Despite the death, the robber was convicted only of aggravated battery and received a

A gargoyle above the entrance to Corpsewood Manor. *Courtesy of Ralph Van Pelt.*

minimal jail sentence. To add insult to injury, he tried to get out of even that on a technicality, though he was unsuccessful.

Charles's mother died in August 1976, and he received a very small inheritance that gave him an income of about $100 per month. Charles's retirement allowance would give them an additional $111 per month. The pair decided to leave "polite" society behind in favor of an alternate civilization of their own creation. They had two huge mastiffs, Beelzebub and Arsinath (whose name was divulged by a friend of the couple and confirmed in writing on the back of a photograph of her at the manor; according to Peter Gilmore, H.P. Lovecraft is a popular author among Satanists, and the dog was probably named after his soul-switching character Asenath Waite). They longed for peace and space where both they and their beloved canines could breathe. They searched high and low for a piece of land totally surrounded by the national forest, isolated from the prying eyes of neighbors and townsfolk, leaving them free to do their own thing without fear of interference from disapproving busybodies.

They failed to take into account, however, that the occasional necessary outside contact, such as shopping trips, would arouse the curious much more in a small town than in a big, anonymous city. It was a fatal mistake.

At last, after scouring several southern states, they got a reply from a seller with a forty-acre tract in the middle of the Chattahoochee National Forest in Trion, Georgia. In 1975, Charles bought the land for a mere $10,500. One source claimed they got the land so cheap because the previous owners, a family named Jackson, had all died from rattlesnake bites after stumbling into a nest of the serpents and that, thereafter, twenty-seven rattlers had been rounded up on the land, allegedly named "Jackson Hollow" after the family. However, this appears to be the stuff of urban legend, as no documentation of such an incident can be found, and the seller's last name was Cooper. Still, a web search revealed there *is* a Jackson Hollow in Chattooga County, though it appears to be closer to Armuchee than Trion.

Charles had a well dug and prepared for the big move. On his fiftieth birthday in 1976, Dr. Scudder resigned from the medical school. Before he left, he appropriated a couple of little items: three vials totaling approximately twelve thousand doses of government-grade LSD-25 and two human skulls. Somehow, the school did not notice their absence. The professor auctioned off almost all his worldly possessions, sold his home and bought a camper, a Jeep and a wood stove. In the middle of a blizzard, they loaded up the Jeep and moved with their two dogs to their enchanted kingdom in the woods.

It has been almost universally reported that Odom and Scudder moved to Georgia in 1976, based in large part on the original *Murder at Corpsewood's* slight misquote of Scudder's *Mother Earth* article that in 1976 he got rid of most of his possessions, arranged for a moving company "*and*" left for Georgia. In fact, the article as originally written reported the things he did in 1976 in one sentence, and "*then,*" according to the next sentence, they left, in the midst of what he referred to as an icy blizzard. A review of weather records that winter indicates that the only East Coast blizzard that he could have been referencing was the blizzard of January 1977, which caused snow and ice from Canada to Florida, freezing Lake Erie solid and famously creating "The Day It Snowed in Miami." It is no surprise, then, that Charles reported terrible conditions from the time they left Chicago until well after they arrived in Georgia.

After many hours of navigating through the driving snow and ice, repeatedly getting lost and spending the night in their vehicle because they could not locate the property once they arrived at the mountain, Charlie and Joey finally reached their dream land, only to be greeted by the rotting, stinking carcass of a deceased horse and an imposing graveyard of denuded trees standing starkly against the sky. Rather than letting the circumstances diminish their dream, they took it in stride with humor, christening the drive "Dead Horse Road" and their future home "Corpsewood Manor."

When the snow finally melted enough for them to again locate the road out, they bought a few items of equipment necessary for building and survival and began the long, slow process of erecting by hand their castle in the woods, despite the fact that neither had any construction experience. In the meantime, they slept first in the Jeep, then in a tent, then in a temporary shelter (possibly the Chicken House). Charles did most of the building, as Joey had injured his leg in a car wreck. The curved walls slowly emerged to grace the meadow like Aphrodite springing from the sea, alien but somehow in harmony with the landscape. Legend says curved walls protect their residents from evil, which has no corner in which to hide. Finally, they got the first floor under cover that summer, allowing them to at long last move into their home. A year later, they had the roof over the second floor and were able to fully occupy their manor, which, despite having no electricity or other utilities, remained relatively comfortable thanks to the cave-like qualities created by the natural insulation of the triple brick wall. A hand pump, candles, stoves with an ample supply of wood and an outhouse provided for free the

Above: The front of Corpsewood Manor, taken during the murder investigation. Note the pink gargoyle over the gazebo entrance. *Bobby Gilliland.*

Left: The triple brick layer of the manor, with insulating space between, helped maintain a comfortable temperature year round. *Amy Petulla.*

conveniences for which most people paid monthly utility bills. They had a small natural pond, which they planned to expand into a large pool. Some of the pipe from that project can still be seen today. The partners created an in-ground cool storage area by burying an old refrigerator; planted fruit trees along with vegetable and rose gardens; ground their own wheat, which they bought for seven dollars per one hundred pounds; built a beehive for honey and beeswax; foraged the forest for other foods; and built and stocked a very special chicken house.

Chapter 3

THE MANOR

The three-story "Chicken House" did indeed stock chickens on the ground floor. The middle floor was used to store canned goods and contained a pornographic library. The upper floor of the Chicken House would ignite talk and speculations for decades. The entire floor consisted of one large room, which Charles and Joey themselves referred to as the "Pink Room." The rest of the world would come to know it as the "Pleasure Chamber."

The Pink Room was, as its name implies, painted entirely pink. The room contained no chairs but instead was stocked with mattresses decked in pink sheets for sitting or reclining. It was clearly not simply for Charles and Joey's entertainment but was an area specifically designed with guests in mind. Lit by candles and oil lamps, it also contained whips, chains and other devices designed for sexual use and primarily gay pornography. Despite the overwhelming curiosity that has always centered on this room, not a single photo can be found of its interior—not in the court file, the crime scene video or even on the Internet.

Besides the sexual content, one additional item in the chamber has generated a tremendous amount of conjecture. A guest book that has frequently been referred to as a diary was kept on the third floor of the Chicken House. Many visitors had signed in to the guest book. Many were from out of town, but a rumor has persisted that there was at least one prominent local resident whose name appeared in the book. Two separate law enforcement sources confirmed that they had seen the book at the time of the investigation and that it did indeed contain such a name. Not only

The infamous Chicken House. The Pink Room, used for entertainment and sexual diversions, was on the third floor. *Bobby Gilliland.*

that, but according to one, the book also contained sexual preferences, and both confirm it held compromising photographs. This particular book has been the source of much speculation. Some deny it ever existed. Many of the lawyers in the murder case claim they never even heard of it. But besides the law enforcement sources mentioned and trial witness Tracey Bell Wilson, one absolutely unimpeachable source confirmed the existence of the diary. Former sheriff Gary McConnell said that the diary was turned in as evidence, and he "had no idea what happened to it after that." Whether it was lost, stolen or destroyed, the diary was never seen again. The missing book was not the only place Scudder kept such information, however. He maintained old letters, notes and even torn slips of paper with information about his visitors and correspondents. Some of these slips contained information on sexual preferences, as well as names and addresses. For example, one slip still in the court file says, "Mr. Jimmy [last name deleted], middle aged, middle income, **leather**, was locked up…10-14- wrote him."

Everyone involved in the investigation seems to have assumed that Charlie and Joey were lovers. After all, they were both gay, they moved to the area together, lived together for twenty-three years and were constantly in each other's company. However, they were never seen demonstrating affection for each other in public, they maintained separate bedrooms and the correspondence and photos found during the investigation left significant doubt as to the nature of their bond. While often referred to as a couple, they clearly did not have a monogamous relationship, and though they shared a bond deeper than many married couples, their close friend Candice Williamson confirmed that they were not paramours in the traditional sense. As she put it in a recent interview, "They may have had sex a few times a month, but they were not a 'couple.'"

Dr. Scudder corresponded with a large number of men. Many, like Joey, were former or even current prisoners, some teachers or models, some teenagers, but the correspondence almost all centered on one thing: sex. Charles Scudder had clearly sent out indiscriminate invitations far and wide to men to come visit, and the desires, acts and body parts described in great detail in these letters from his correspondents left no doubt about the purpose of the proposed visits. Nowhere in any of the numerous letters does it appear that Charles ever so much as mentioned Joey to these potential sex partners. Many of the responses included explicit nude photos of the pen pals. There were also photos that were clearly taken during Playtime at Corpsewood. Mark Fults, a local psychic and author familiar with the pair from his contact with the "Brookwood Satanists" the roommates welcomed into their lives, has speculated that Scudder's vision of the needs and feelings of others was overshadowed by his own desires, leading him to often leave Joey in the background and indulge his own sex drive whenever and wherever that drive led him and with whomever was led to visit at Corpsewood. And visit they did.

The residents of Corpsewood Manor had frequent visitors. According to two witnesses, the couple threw "Sex and Game" parties, during which participants enjoyed sex, Scudder's potent homemade wine and possibly LSD. According to the investigator who had read some of the diary, party guests were asked to arrive a few days before the main activities would commence, and Dr. Scudder would perform a medical exam of sorts to ensure guests were in fit health to indulge in the proffered entertainment and libations. The diary contained medical notes from these exams on several entries. The fact that his was not a medical doctorate seemed to deter them not at all. These guests generally spent their time in the Pink Room or the woods. Attorney Ben Ballenger, who would later be appointed to represent Kenneth Brock, tells of an occasion in his youth when he and a friend rode their motorcycle up the mountain to Corpsewood to check it out. They found "a bunch of college kids in white robes" who appeared quite stoned on some type of drug outside the manor.

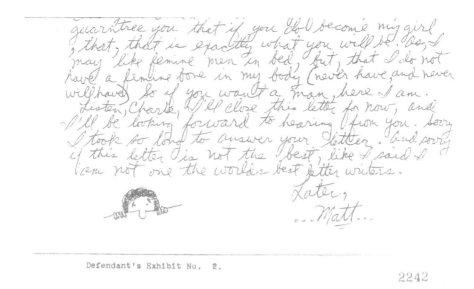

guarantee you that if you ___ become my girl
, that, that is exactly what you will be. As, I
may like femine men in bed, but, that I do not
have a femine bone in my body (never have, and never
will have) So if you want a man, here I am.
Listen, Charlie, I'll close this letter for now, and
I'll be looking forward to hearing from you. Sorry
I took so long to answer your letter. And sorry
if this letter is not the best, like I said I
am not one the worlds best letter writers.

Later,
...Matt...

Defendant's Exhibit No. 2.

2242

An excerpt from one of the less explicit letters from one of Charles Scudder's prison pen pals. *Tony West exhibit file.*

It should be remembered that LSD was initially thought to have the potential for psychotherapeutic effects. The drug was invented in 1938 by Dr. Albert Hofmann from ergot fungus derived from rye grain and was first commercially released in 1947 by Sandoz Laboratories. It was not always seen as the scourge many believe it to be today, now that its potential for long-term and unpredictable effects has been revealed. It was not made illegal by the United States until late 1968, and even then, studies of LSD in human patients continued through the 1980s. Some contend experiments to find medical uses for the substance continue today. It was a legal prescription drug in Switzerland as late as 1993. Famed psychologist Timothy Leary was doing experiments with hallucinogens at Harvard University and touting the benefits of LSD, urging people to "turn on, tune in, drop out" and "think for yourself and question authority." Particularly among intellectuals, the drug was as likely to be viewed with amusement as scorn. Thus, Scudder was not as likely to have the vociferous negative attitude about the substance that many of his current advocates adopt when denying its presence there.

LSD increases the signal to serotonin receptors and is thought to inhibit the firing of certain types of cells, in part by decreasing the activity of inhibitory transmitter 5-hydroxytryptamine, thus making certain neurons more active. This causes the user to pick up more stimuli, including minute environmental factors hitherto unnoticed, and the overwhelmed senses can result in hallucination. It can also cause communication between parts of the brain that don't normally connect, resulting in mixed senses, such as tasting colors (synesthesia). Some sources advance the theory that because certain functions of the brain are inhibited by LSD use, the mind creates new synapses and new ways to interpret stimuli, resulting in altered perception. The involved systems affect sensation, perception, mood, attention and sleep. The effects most widely described are visual hallucinations: walls "melting," patterns appearing or moving, colors looking brighter, lights glowing, sensing in what has been described as another dimension. Logical thinking also seems to be affected in a way that can cause judgment calls that do not seem to be in keeping with the user's typical morality. For example, one user described how he could not conceive that someone would not give water to another person in need, and the fact that the shop where water was available was closed did not factor into the equation at all. Another had no interspecies concerns with being in love with his fish. This type of thinking was temporary for these users. The effect on mood seems largely dependent on the user's surroundings; those who use the drug while in an uncomfortable situation or who find themselves having to interact with people they feel would not approve of the use of the drug are more likely to have a "bad trip" characterized by paranoia and anxiety. Reports of such negative reactions appear to be relatively rare, however. The vast majority of users who speak of their trips publicly report positive experiences. While there are very few people who have reported using such a substance at Corpsewood, and many contend that there are credibility issues surrounding those who have, none claimed to have been given the drug without their knowledge or reported negative reactions except for the criminals, who obviously had reason to lie, and Tracey Bell Wilson, who testified to a history of mental illness.

As word got around about the two "devil worshippers" who lived in a castle with no utilities in the middle of the woods, curious locals also came to visit. One witness described how, if an unknown guest dropped by at night, rather than saying, "Who are you?" as most would, Dr. Scudder would call out, "Who am I?" If the visitor knew his hosts by name, he was welcomed.

Guests arriving in the daytime were generally greeted while still in their car by the two enormous guard dogs. All who encountered the dogs claim they were the size of small ponies. According to Sheriff's Deputy Bobby Gilliland, who was one of the curious who dropped by for a chat one day in 1981, Scudder told him the canine sentries were trained to allow people who came by when he and Joey were not home to get out of the car. However, once they were out, they would find that the dogs had positioned themselves between the visitors and their cars, so they had no retreat should the animals find it necessary to attack. Was this simply a tale created to prevent strangers from exploring when the lords of the manor were away? Possibly, though it seems an odd thing to tell a pair of uniformed officers sitting in a police car. However, it was said in a friendly tone. Like everyone else, Bobby found Charles to be polite, friendly and charming and Joey to be quiet but a bit unfocused. Joey had suffered significant brain damage when their vehicle wrecked shortly after the pair moved to Georgia and, according to Bobby, seemed to have a hard time following a train of thought, which could account for some of his reticence. He came out that day, as he often did with drop-in visitors, to bum a cigarette. While not demonstrably affectionate, the pair let male visitors know they were gay, in case they were interested in a more intimate visit, but if not, assured the men that no one would bother them. This seems to belie later accusations that they were out to take advantage of unsuspecting straight men.

Ben Ballenger, likewise, found Charles to be gracious on the occasion he visited. The professor's Jeep pulled up after they arrived, frightening Ben's friend so badly that he ran off and hid. When Dr. Scudder asked if he could help them, Ben quickly said that they were just interested in the "Beware of the Thing" sign. Dr. Scudder, who was clearly used to curious strangers and their excuses, simply smiled and asked whether his friend (whom he had spotted in his rapid retreat to conceal himself) was all right.

So why would these two who had relocated to the Deep South in search of privacy welcome strangers so warmly? Theories vary widely. Some would contend it was a simple matter of good manners, the inherent southern hospitality that apparently came naturally to these northerners. Some say that Scudder supplemented his income by selling his wine, and as with any other sales-based business, graciousness helped expand his customer base. But those who knew the professor best all say he was a brilliant and curious man who was both fascinated and amused by the intricacies of human behavior, and this innate curiosity quite conceivably was at the heart of this cordiality.

More than one person has claimed that Scudder told them he was continuing his experiments from Loyola on people he met in Chattooga County. They generally have assumed he meant experiments with drugs, and religious conservatives have trumpeted that contention in support of their assertions that Scudder was a fiend. But such assumptions fly in the face of two very important facts. First, later scientific tests in the criminal case showed the wine was *not* drugged as the killers had alleged. Just as important, Charles Scudder's intellectual and professional pursuits in the field of psychology were not limited simply to drugs but also behavior.

Dr. Scudder published prodigiously within his fields of expertise. He wrote on everything from the effect of electroshock on behavior and amino acid levels in mice and "The Brain: A Neurohumerally Regulated Ultrahomeostat" to an essay on the dangers of preservatives, to a spoof paper on "A Study on the Activity, Ethology and Psychology of Fluorescent Plastic Cubes," satirically positing that plastic cubes demonstrated behavior when presented with the stimulus of mice. He was intensely interested in human behavior and not above making provocative statements just to see what reaction he would get. Some claim he acknowledged occasionally doing exactly that. While he enjoyed his privacy, it would be erroneous to say he wanted to be left completely alone. Scudder sometimes liked prodding at people's psyches the same way some little boys like poking a snake or other potentially dangerous animal with a stick, what is sometimes referred to as "waking the dragon." He wanted to know what made people tick. He enjoyed honing his ability to shape behavior, and the myriad guests who arrived in his drive gave him plenty of opportunity to do exactly that. So when guests came calling during daylight hours, Dr. Charles Scudder was always happy to step out of his home and converse with them.

Very few visitors were invited into the manor itself, though it was the subject of overwhelming speculation. The oval brick structure was only forty-four by sixteen feet, with a retractable drawbridge connecting the main house to a sundeck above the entrance gazebo, where they enjoyed taking tea. One source said that Zeke Woodall, who befriended the pair, told him before his own death that they actually maintained their altar on this sundeck. Some have questioned the existence of an altar, contending that if Scudder was indeed an atheistic Satanist, an altar would be incongruous. However, Anton LaVey, the founder of the Church of Satan, came from a carny background and had a deep appreciation of the theatrical. He suggested the use of props such as an altar, bell (like the one purchased by George C. Coker from their estate), candles (like those found all over their home), the Sigil of Baphomet (discussed in more detail later), medallions (such as the one Tony West admired around Charles Scudder's neck shortly before he snuffed out his life) and a sword (such as the one that can be seen in the photo of their Baphomet, on page 43) when performing "Greater Magic," which current High Priest Peter Gilmore describes as "a form of cathartic ritual experience" or "controlled fantasy for emotional release."

Corpsewood, with the drawbridge down to connect the independent gazebo tower to the house. *Courtesy of Ralph Van Pelt.*

Downstairs, there was a kitchen and a dining area that led to the library. This library, where Dr. Scudder kept his desk, was filled with books on a large variety of subjects, including the occult, cybernetics, psychopharmacology, works of fiction and Dr. Scudder's own papers. Some of these books were salvaged and still exist today. Many contain the professor's handwritten notes, and a faint whiff of wood smoke from the manor's heat source still lingers. Contrary to many rumors, the home had no basement, and there was no underground lab anywhere on the property.

Upstairs, they each had a bedroom, as well as a small hall with the door to the drawbridge. Dr. Scudder owned a golden harp that he sometimes played from the tower deck at night, when the full moon would reflect the moonlight from their pond onto the pink gargoyle, purportedly making it glow neon. The unearthly tones seemed to draw forth a time when castles, lords and magic might be waiting behind every hill.

The house was filled with renaissance-era furniture that had previously occupied the Chicago mansion. The furnishings sat amid the woods for months, covered in plastic, awaiting the warm embrace of the castle sanctuary. The beautiful carved antique furniture was not the most unusual thing in the home, however. The house was filled, top to bottom, with Satanic

The statue of Mephistopheles. This statue was given as partial payment for attorney's fees after the murders to famed attorney Bobby Lee Cook. *Courtesy of Ralph Van Pelt.*

art. The most famous piece of art from the home was a black and gold statue of Mephistopheles, a demonic being associated with, and sometimes interchanged with, the Christian Satan. Since their deaths, many people sympathetic to the couple, though they never knew them, have asserted that Scudder was at most a pagan being falsely accused of Satanist leanings and that his only sin was being gay in rural Georgia. I was one of those people. I was wrong.

It should be noted first that the 1980s was a time when "Satanic Panic" was at its height. Fundamentalist Christians were seeing signs of "devil worship" everywhere, reminiscent of the McCarthy-era communist "Red Scare" witch hunts. From heavy metal music to teens playing dungeons and dragons to supposed secret signs in the logos of large international companies, it seemed as though there was a Satanist hiding behind every corner. Some have asserted this was caused by the intersection of a strong interest in the paranormal, as illustrated by the popularity of such movies as the *Halloween*, *Amityville* and *Poltergeist* series; songs like "Thriller" (released less than two weeks before the tragic events at Corpsewood); and the rise of conservative politics and organizations like the Parents Music Resource Center, which was responsible for putting labels on albums warning against profanity and the like. This panic culminated with the infamous McMartin Preschool case, where the school's director, her son and some teachers at the school were accused of molesting forty children, making pornographic movies of the youngsters and using them in Satanic rituals, including sex with animals and several alleged animal and even human baby sacrifice rituals. The children also said they were molested by Santa Claus, were flushed down toilets to arrive at a location where they were molested and witnessed flying witches, among other things. The accusations led to the defendants being charged with 208 counts of child abuse. In a move evocative of the Salem witch trials, defendants were offered deals if they would confess their Satanic acts. None did. Despite extensive searches, no physical evidence was found, and after one of the longest and most expensive trials in American history, the defendants were acquitted on all counts. Satanic Panic gradually died down, although it still occasionally raises its head, as in current accusations that the claw-mark symbol of a certain energy drink is actually the diabolical "666" and a giant coffee company's symbol is secretly somehow the insignia of the Church of Satan. Clearly, thousands of people and organizations have been falsely accused of Satanic acts and associations. That, however, does not negate the fact that there was and is indeed a Church of Satan with a significant number of followers, if not the masses that were denounced in the panic. Most have not engaged in the violent acts contemplated by those accusers in the '80s. But many who wish to be "explorers on the untrodden paths of science, human motivation and mystery—all that is most truly occult" (as the CoS puts it on its website) consider themselves disciples.

Joey Odom and Charles Scudder may have been good, kind, polite men who would never harm a fly. They may have generously shared what they had and wished only to live life on their own terms. They may have endured prejudice for their differences. But Charles Scudder, at least, was without a doubt a card-carrying member of the Church of Satan.

Besides the Mephistopheles statue, many other such dark items and symbols filled the house. Many allegedly were former props of the Balaban and Katz Chicago Theatre, bought in a liquidation sale. Two horned, fanged statues presided over the bed. The four chimneys were decorated with pentacles (pentagrams, or five-pointed stars, enclosed by a circle) with their points down. Their Jeep was also conspicuously marked with large upside-down pentacles on the doors. Eliphas Levi, an occult author and self-proclaimed ceremonial magician, tells us in *Transcendental Magic, Its Doctrine and Ritual* (1854), "A reversed pentagram, with two points projecting upwards, is a symbol of evil and attracts sinister forces because it overturns the proper order of things and demonstrates the triumph of matter over spirit. It is the goat of lust attacking the heavens with its horns, a sign execrated by initiates." Others say the inversion represents Lucifer's fall. Dr. Scudder had also created and displayed his own Satanic art. One was a stained-glass Baphomet, or goat's head pentacle.

The Sigil of Baphomet is the official symbol and trademark of the Church of Satan. It appeared on the Satanic Bible in 1969, following its first appearance on the church's Satanic Mass record in 1968. The Baphomet is a point-down five-pointed star that has been converted into a goat's head, with the horns as the top two points, the ears as the side points and the chin as the bottom point, all enclosed in a circle. Beneath the Baphomet was, as one prosecutor described it, "a small ritual cabinet containing teddy bears." It is unknown how the bears were used; however, those who visited the manor as children report they never saw the bears, and the stuffed animals did not appear to have been used as toys for the dogs. Interestingly, this cabinet was located quite close to the drawbridge leading to the sundeck where one witness said they used their altar. A winged mirror in the professor's bedroom may have represented another Baphomet, which in full form was depicted with wings to designate him as a fallen angel. Another piece of Scudder's stained glass depicted a Medusa-like skull. Paintings on either

The four chimneys of Corpsewood Manor, replete with downward-facing pentacles. *Courtesy of Ralph Van Pelt.*

A stained-glass Baphomet created by Charles Scudder, with teddy bear cabinet below, close to the drawbridge door. A sword is leaning against the scrollwork. *Courtesy of Ralph Van Pelt.*

Left: A stained-glass Medusa skull created by Charles Scudder. *Courtesy of Ralph Van Pelt.*

Below: Birth and death baby paintings by Charles Scudder flanked the entrance to the spiral staircase in Corpsewood Manor. *Courtesy of Ralph Van Pelt.*

One of the law enforcement officials described this as an original Satanic Bible. *Courtesy of Ralph Van Pelt.*

side of the spiral staircase depicted a baby emerging from the womb on the left and the same baby in a mirror position, but dead and skeletonized, on the right. These paintings concealed cabinets where the dishes were kept. However, behind the shelves holding everyday dishes was another hidden door, cloaking a number of items of silver, whose presence was revealed only to a chosen few. Finally, an old, worn Satanic Bible was kept in a place of honor. While rumors have circulated that this book was bound in human skin, there has never been any evidence to support that.

Chapter 4

The Church of Satan

On what wings dare he aspire?
What the hand, dare seize the fire?…
What the anvil? what dread grasp,
Dare its deadly terrors clasp!

When the stars threw down their spears
And water'd heaven with their tears:
Did he smile his work to see?
Did he who made the Lamb make thee?

Tyger Tyger burning bright,
In the forests of the night:
What immortal hand or eye,
Dare frame thy fearful symmetry?[*]
—William Blake, "The Tyger," 1794

---

[*] After the initial draft containing this entire quote was turned in, the documentary *Corpsewood*, by WGGS Dove Broadcasting (1984), came to light. The initial creators of the documentary intended to create a balanced account of the Corpsewood story. However, when Joanne Thompson took over the production, it instead went galloping down a narrow one-way track of right wing religious rhetoric. It has never aired in Georgia and only became available on YouTube in November 2015. Although the documentary is wildly prejudicial and speculative, it has one extraordinary redeeming feature: it contains audiotape of Charles Scudder made by Raymond Williams on the last day of Scudder's life, playing his harp while reciting poetry—specifically, the bolded lines above. The author had no knowledge that Dr. Scudder had ever recited these lines, much less in an audiotape on the day of his death, at the time this quote was originally selected and included as the perfect quotation for this book.

The Church of Satan website claims William Blake as its poet and forbear, acknowledging the respect they both share for knowledge that leads to power and appreciation of the sensual here-and-now. Although he claimed to love Christ, Blake says in his poem "The Everlasting Gospel" (circa 1818):

> *The Vision of Christ that thou dost See*
> *Is my Visions Greatest Enemy...*
> *Both read the Bible day & night*
> *But thou readst black where I read White.*

His "Proverbs of Hell" further set out beliefs since adopted by the CoS:

> *The road of excess leads to the palace of wisdom.*
> *He who desires but acts not, breeds pestilence...*
> *As the caterpillar chooses the fairest leaves to lay her eggs on, so the priest*
> *lays his curse on the fairest joys...*
> *Sooner murder an infant in its cradle than nurse unacted desires.*

Contrary to what most people believe, members of the Church of Satan are not "devil worshippers" but, rather, atheists who worship no god but instead revel in indulging all the base yearnings of the body. According to this "church," men celebrate their own divinity by enjoying worldly pleasures. They strive to harness the full potential of the mind and universe for their own use. Charles Scudder was heard to say that he was not a follower of Christianity, as there was no power in it. The Church of Satan certainly holds out the offer of power to gain one's desires.

It is no great surprise, given their philosophies, that the self-indulgent Church of Satan was founded by Anton LaVey in the tumultuous, "If it feels good, do it" 1960s. Specifically, it was founded at midnight on the dawn of the auspicious May Day (May 1) 1966 in San Francisco. It is interesting to note that the Society for Creative Anachronism (SCA) was founded the exact same day, a few miles away in Berkeley. The society is the group known for reverting to the Middle Ages by dressing in medieval garb and cavorting in the woods or, if one can be found, a castle, eschewing modern conveniences and utilities, often drinking homemade wine and incorporating period items, like harps or even renaissance furniture, into their revelries. Many also eschew Christianity in favor of pagan rites that they believe were practiced during that era.

Sound familiar? It could not be determined whether Charles Scudder participated in the SCA, due in large part to the fact that SCA members operate under different character names and usually do not share their actual identities. Without a doubt, though, one of Scudder's sons has been a very active member of the SCA for decades. Besides sharing a founding date, calendar (beginning for both on their founding date, year I AS) and initials with the Church of Satan (which is referred to by some as the Satanic Church or the Satanic Church of America), the SCA surely shared some founding members, as both drew alienated college students from the Berkeley/San Francisco area.

The relationship between Charles Scudder and Church of Satan founder Anton LaVey has been the subject of widespread conjecture. After the murders, LaVey vehemently denied that he had visited Scudder at Corpsewood, as has often been claimed; however, he *did* send Scudder a birthday card on behalf of the church not long before the professor's death. Many sources claim that the card was for Scudder's fifty-sixth birthday, although a few note with puzzlement that the card said it was for his sixteenth birthday. In fact, the Church of Satan turned sixteen the year of Scudder's death, so most likely, the card was celebrating that anniversary rather than a natal event. Sadly, that card has mysteriously disappeared from the court file, along with several other documents. One document that does still remain is a letter from one of his prison pen pals, which makes clear that Charles mentioned the Church of Satan's Baphomet insignia in his ad in the *Gay Community News* for such pen pals: "I was just reading the GCN...I like the way your ad is written. I can't understand a damn thing on it but your name, a part of it anyway. (Smile) I don't know if Corpsewood is your last name or the name of the street you live on. 'Those who bear the great seal of oaphomet [*sic*].' What is 'seal of oaphomet??'" Furthermore, his correspondence with another prisoner revealed that Charles had upbraided the man for sending a religious Thanksgiving card, as the inmate covered half a page apologizing repeatedly for offending him by sending something religious, calling Charles a "spitfire" for his reaction. The highest and best proof that Charles Scudder was a Satanist, however, is not found in the court file. Magus Peter H. Gilmore, current high priest of the Church of Satan, recently confirmed Scudder's membership in the organization. Furthermore, bank records found at the house revealed several checks written to the Church of Satan.

Although they do not believe in a god, the Church of Satan does believe that, with the proper knowledge and rituals, their members can do what they refer to as "magic." Some groups calling themselves

A magical hand gesture found in the Necronomicon allegedly translated by famed alchemist Dr. John Dee, bound by the reclaiming vines of Corpsewood. *Jon Dennis.*

"Satanic" have committed terrible acts, claiming they do so in an attempt to increase their power and cast spells. In 2014, self-proclaimed Satanist and devil worshipper Gregory Scott Hale murdered, dismembered and partially ate Chattanooga resident Marie Hyder for that very reason. The Church of Satan, however, points out that it does not worship the devil or any other entity and distinguishes that while devil worshippers choose to follow the path of God's adversary and adopt anti-Christian behavior and values, Satanists value that which benefits them, but not at the expense of others.

Occasionally, you will hear Church of Satan members referred to as "LaVeyan" (after their founder, Anton LaVey) or "symbolic Satanists" to distinguish from actual devil worshippers who call themselves Satanists. Charles Scudder fell in the LaVeyan camp. In contrast, back in the 1960s and '70s, a group known as the "Brookwood Satanists," named after the Brookwood Apartments off Dayton Boulevard in a Chattanooga suburb known as Red Bank, practiced a style of "sorcery" that was definitely at the expense of others. According to paranormal expert Mark Fults, they were led by a man who went by various names, but most commonly Bill Odom, who owned a shop called Witches' Rings and Magick Things in a house on Dayton Boulevard across from Cooley's Formalwear. The house still stands today, but although it is kept up, no one seems to live there. A chain across the stairs to the door proclaiming "Private Property" prevents entrance. Odom furnished his followers with hashish, acid and sex. As time passed, they became more sexual and sadistic and attempted to carry out a very dark "magic" in the house. According to Mark, members of the Brookwood Satanists claimed to have practiced human sacrifice on more than one occasion, using as victims homeless people in the area whose absence was not likely to be noted by authorities. Some claimed they witnessed their leader levitate a large rock through the house. The members of the group are all dead now, but Mark states that members he knew claimed to have been regular visitors at Corpsewood during Joey and Charlie's residence in Trion. Falsely implying they were LaVeyan Satanists rather than the devil worshippers they truly were, could they have persuaded the intellectually curious professor to try out some of their spells?*

One of the most notorious magic spells among those who accept magic as real is the summoning of demons. It is occasionally whispered that Charles said he had invoked a demon, which he carried with him. A sign reminiscent of *The Addams Family* was posted on the drive leading to Corpsewood, reading, "Beware of the Thing." Most thought this referred to one of the mastiffs, but certain superstitious souls are convinced he was referring instead to this demon. According to Fults, if the man did attempt to invoke a demon, it most likely was a guardian for the castle and property. Mark states that Scudder, though, was an "intellectual Satanist"—he learned about the Church of Satan, adopted the symbols, enjoyed the scandal associated with being a so-called devil worshipper and may have dabbled at casting spells

---

* You can read more about the Brookwood Satanists in Mark's book *Chattanooga Chills*.

The former Witches' Rings and Magick Things building, reflected in the window of the shop directly across the street. *Amy Petulla.*

and the like, without really taking it too seriously, so these rumors are likely unfounded. However, those who believe the place is cursed often attribute it to this creature. Perhaps those rumors are what led the police to statements they would later make when the shadow of evil fell on Corpsewood after Tony West and Kenneth Avery Brock came calling. But until then, life in Trion was bliss.

Chapter 5

LIFE IN TRION

Charles Scudder and Joseph Odom had a loving relationship, which was demonstrated in many different ways, in life and death. Initially, as he had in Chicago, Joey served as housekeeper and cook. But in 1977, Charles (according to legal staff; friends tell a different story) was driving their automobile with Odom at his side when the Jeep went out of control and wrecked. A witness who happened by that day said the vehicle did not appear to have sustained much damage, but vehicles at that time were built quite solidly so they would resist damage on impact, without the "crumple zones" found in today's automobiles. Unfortunately, the result was that the energy from a collision continued through the car until it found a movable object where it could dissipate—usually, the passengers. Thus, while older cars held up better in wrecks, their passengers suffered the consequences, whereas contemporary cars will absorb the energy so that the auto body sustains the damage rather than the people within.

Joey received the brunt of the impact and sustained a leg injury and serious brain damage. He was a convalescent for at least a year afterward. During that time, Dr. Scudder cared for his needs instead, waiting on him hand and foot, providing medical care and arranging for Joe's disability claim through the law offices of Bryant Henry and Jon Wood in Lafayette. Thanks to Charles's tender ministrations, Joey gradually healed, but the brain injury left some lasting damage. He had always been the quiet one of the pair, in contrast to Charlie's extroverted enthusiasm, so often his tendency to get sidetracked and inability to follow a conversation went unnoticed.

Their time was their own, and the two partners relished the ability to enjoy life on their terms. While building their castle was hard work, tending the gardens, the vineyards and the beehives was a source of joy rather than a cause for complaint, as were the other labors attendant to their self-sustaining lifestyle: making candles and wine, cutting wood, cooking on the old-fashioned stove, feeding the chickens and the like. According to the criminal investigators who came later, cleaning was not high on their priority list, so it was sometimes neglected in favor of more pleasurable pursuits, such as playing the harp, as well as enjoying and sharing the wine and sex that had become an important part of their lifestyle.

Despite the fact that their intention was to keep under the radar, they did develop relationships and friendships with a few of the locals. One of their closest friends was Candice Williamson. She was a frequent visitor to the manor. On pretty days, she, Joey, Charles and her children would sit outside at the picnic table in the back, enjoying the pastoral surroundings. Candice's daughter Kerri Hamilton remembers Corpsewood as an "almost magical place." The colors and scents surrounding the house were so vivid, they remain etched in her memory to this day, as do the flavors of the blackberry dessert Joey would make and the sound of Charles playing the harp. According to Candice, when the children got too wild, the only thing that could quiet them was the sound of Charles's music. He and Joey were both very patient and sweet with the kids. Joey, in fact, kept Raggedy Ann and Andy dolls on his bed at one time, which one of the people who visited as a child remembered fondly. The family recalled one of the chickens was crippled and walked with a limp, which had transformed it into a pet.

The only things Kerri found a little scary at the castle were the dogs, and that was simply because of their size. Many, including Kerri, have remarked that the larger dog, Beelzebub, was so big that he could stick his head in a car window or the back of a Jeep while standing on four legs. District Attorney Investigator Johnny Bass recalls that when he and Richard Dye went out to the property while it was still under construction to investigate the wreck, one of the dogs approached his vehicle carrying a car tire in its mouth like a chew toy and pressed its nose up against the window.

The couple welcomed Candice and her family like long-lost friends. They were part of the inner circle who were welcomed into the manor itself—never the Chicken House. While the children played, Candice and Charles would drink wine, play chess and chat. The atmosphere was warm, friendly and relaxed, the kind of ambiance found among close family members who enjoyed each other's company. Candice confirmed that Charles threw many parties, including weddings, in that idyllic setting, surrounded by nature in all its glorious splendor. As she and Charles both enjoyed reading, they would often trade books. They shared an appreciation for a wide variety of reading material, everything from history to Stephen King. This shared love of reading led to hour upon hour of conversation about books and thoughts and dreams. Candice described her friend as one who tried to better himself his whole life. She thought of Charles almost as a big brother, looking out for her and giving her advice. He likewise confided in her. Candice was one of the few people who realized that Charles's hair was not naturally blond; it was dark, and he started dyeing it blond when it developed gray as he aged. She was one of his only close "manor" friends who heard him confirm his Satanist beliefs. He also confided to her that he had tasted rat when he cooked up some of his lab animals before, and when looking for reading material one evening, he casually revealed the keyhole drawer where the LSD was kept.

According to Candice, however, the man was not fond of drugs himself. When he was hospitalized with a hernia on the eve of her surprise twenty-fifth birthday party, he waited just long enough to make sure he could make it without medication before checking himself out against medical advice in order to finish the party preparations. When asked about it later, he said that drugs could cause you to "run your mouth about your personal life." Without a doubt, the professor had secrets he guarded carefully from strangers.

There are those who say that Dr. Scudder shared his LSD with a certain subset of his friends. Primarily, these rumors are spread by those who heard about it from what they read online or what they heard from a friend of a friend of a friend. However, after extensive searching, I found one witness whose background and place in the community render him highly reliable who said that he had occasion to interview the president of a motorcycle chapter in the area about the pair shortly after their deaths. According to this man, Charles both shared his acid at parties when the motorcycle leader claimed to be present and sold some of the substance to some of the bikers. The bikers, in turn, felt protective of Dr. Scudder and felt guilty that they had let him down by failing to protect their benefactor from the evil that befell him and Joey. The club members almost all had nicknames, and the leader said the professor had adopted "Scud" as his handle. Interestingly, Charles's father had been called "Scud" by his college fraternity brothers. The witness went on to say that he found the biker credible because he would quote "Scud" using the same speech patterns and phrases he had heard from another close friend of the professor, Raymond Williams, when Raymond quoted Dr. Scudder.

It should be noted that there is a segment of their manor friends who insist that not only did Charles not do drugs himself, but he was also adamantly opposed to the use of drugs and said that drugs were responsible for the downfall of young people. This seems at odds with the three vials of government-labeled LSD 25 found in the manor, half gone. Furthermore, Zeke Woodall said that at Corpsewood parties in the Chicken House, people would drink wine, smoke pot and have sex. Scudder at the very least clearly had no problem with sharing his potent wine with teens.

There is some indication that, while he did not miss his college students, Charles Scudder did miss the joy of shaping young minds. According to Sheriff Gary McConnell, the professor applied to teach at Trion School. He was not hired, however, because the school felt he was overqualified. This did not seem to overly disturb him, though, and he kept his intellect stimulated through reading, conversing and observing the behavior and reactions of others.

Dr. Scudder liked routines, such as dining at precisely 5:00 p.m. every day, and he and Joey quickly fell into the habit of visiting what is now Ronnie's Grocery on Mountain View Road, the road leading to the mountain, every eighteen days like clockwork. They would pick up their mail there, and the folks who worked in the store came to expect their visits. Among the other locals they became familiar with were a couple of close neighbors, along with Tracey Wilson, the daughter of the Lyerly police chief, and Raymond Williams, who visited them regularly. They also frequently welcomed complete strangers, those who enjoyed an alternate lifestyle, societal rejects like those who had served time and others who came to party with them. Among those who had enjoyed their hospitality were Kenneth Brock and Tony West.

Chapter 6

THE KILLERS

Kenneth Avery Brock was seventeen in 1982. He had, in his own words and spelling in a recent letter to the author, "never been to a professional sporting event, nor a live concert, never eaten in a restorant, never had a job were I drew a paycheck were they took out taxes, never filed for my taxes, never had a drivers lisence. Never been married, never had kids, never been to a prom, never had a life nor the chance to learn how to live life, don't know what its like to be love by a woman."

Brock's life had not been easy. He had been abused and ultimately kicked out by his father and began stealing just to eat. As his niece Lin Gray put it, "Tony [West] took him under his wing—the wing of a bat out of hell." Kenneth (often known then as Avery) had no adult convictions at the time. The young man was occasionally employed hauling logs, so he was familiar with the national forest property in Trion. Brock had met Charles Scudder and Joey Odom while hunting deer on their property in the fall of that year. The teen had, of course, heard about the gay devil worshippers who lived in a castle in the woods; unlike the adults in the area, local teenagers knew the couple was free with sharing their wine and, according to some, drugs. Unknown to their parents, a number of the neighboring young people partied at Corpsewood. Dr. Scudder was known to make a potent muscadine wine, which they bottled in glass flasks. The pair invited Brock up to the Pink Room of the Chicken House, which was reached by a ladder scaling the side of the building. Brock was no stranger to drinking, but the powerful, intoxicating beverage loosened his inhibitions somewhat more than he was expecting.

When Charlie performed oral sex on him, Brock did nothing to stop him. The act was technically illegal, but not because Brock was underage. The age of consent in Georgia at the time was just fourteen. Nevertheless, even plain vanilla sex between consenting adults was illegal unless they were married to each other, and all forms of sodomy, including oral sex, even within a marriage, violated the law. While he would later express embarrassment and anger over the encounter, it did not keep the teen from returning for more visits and more sexual encounters. He was accompanied on the last couple of visits before the fateful night by his roommate, Tony West.

Kenneth Avery Brock's booking photo. *Chattooga County Sheriff's Office.*

Samuel Tony West's record was far from spotless. He had shot and killed his two-year-old nephew, Horace Lee Haygood, when he was around thirteen years old while playing with a loaded gun. He deliberately pointed the weapon at the child's head and pulled the trigger, though he later claimed the death was an accident because he did not know the gun was loaded and was just trying to show the toddler that there was "nothing to fear." According to a blog post alleged to have been written by his first cousin, West was then sent to a mental institution until he was eighteen. Whether or not this was correct, West acknowledged at trial that he had received psychological or psychiatric treatment at least fifty or sixty times, so like Hayward Bissell, who would terrorize Trion residents later, mental illness may have heightened an existing ruthless streak. His sister Myra Haygood would later testify that West had "never been the same" after his father died tragically in a train mishap when he was ten. His prospects were no better after he was released from treatment. Numerous posts to a variety of blogs by others claiming to also be family members denounce West as having been a bad seed ever since that original shooting. Just a few years before his fateful encounter with the residents of Corpsewood, he shot his

Tony West at the time of his booking. *Chattooga County Sheriff's Office.*

brother-in-law after escaping from jail, where he was serving a sentence for theft. At age thirty, he was unemployed with a violent felony record, and his prospects were not good. In an effort to conserve what little money he had, he decided to take in a roommate.

Kenneth Brock moved into Tony West's derelict trailer in the late fall of 1982. Brock told his roommate about the queer devil worshippers who were happy to share their wine with friends and strangers alike. Never one to turn down a free high, West visited nearby Corpsewood with Brock one evening to partake of a little complimentary alcohol. Then, as West put it, Scudder "had homosexuality with Avery. And then he reached over to have it with me, and I told him I didn't believe in it, and I wasn't brought up that way, and I left." Afterward, the roommates started discussing the possibilities offered by two gay men who were obviously rich because, after all, they lived in a castle, isolated in the middle of the woods, where no one could hear them scream. The more they talked, the more the idea of a robbery appealed to them. The more Brock thought about those "queers" taking advantage of him, as he had by then convinced himself was the case, the more justified the idea seemed.

So they began plotting. West's initial plan was simply for a robbery. But just as it did for Judy Neelley, Brock's teenage rage escalated with each trip to Trion, and that rage deepened the hues of his cruelty to a much richer palette. Practice their perverted sex on him, would they? Scudder would think twice about that when they raped him with a red-hot soldering iron to force him to tell them where the money was kept!

In early December 1982, Brock went on a reconnaissance mission. The two were familiar with the Chicken House and the infamous Pink Room, but they had never been in the castle itself, so they had no idea where the valuables were. While it might be more fun to torture the answer out of their victims, it was certainly more expedient if they already knew where to find the goods. The pair soon found that was easier said than done, however. Brock showed up for a tryst, but when he asked to go inside the manor, Scudder firmly refused. They may have been hospitable to strangers and friends alike, but their home was, after all, their castle, and only a select few were allowed in there. Had he gained admittance, the conspirators might have realized at least one of the flaws in their plan. Perhaps they thought it was only the Chicken House that did not have electricity, or perhaps, in their alcohol-induced stupor, they never even realized that there was in fact no power in that structure or believed it was lit with candles and heated with a wood stove simply for ambiance. Regardless, their plan with the soldering iron (which they did not even have but thought for some reason they could find at the manor) was a poor one, given that electricity is necessary to heat the tool. So Brock went home that night unsatisfied, at least from an informational standpoint.

There was at least one further problem with their plan. Although they lived in a small castle on a large tract of land without working at paying jobs, and although Scudder had previously made enough as a professor to enable him to live in a decaying Chicago mansion, the pair kept literally no cash on hand. If they went to the market for so much as one of the thirty-seven-cent Eskimo Pies they loved, they would write a check. Every cent they owned was kept in the bank and meticulously accounted for. Charles had approximately $40,000 from his pension and sale of the Chicago home, after the purchase of the land and all materials necessary to build the castle. They kept that money in a joint savings account and T-bills, which paid them approximately $200 per month interest. Other than a bit they made from selling their excellent wine and, according to some, other recreational intoxicants, that $200 represented their entire monthly budget, and even those funds were kept in a small checking account for their day-to-day expenses. Had the bandits bothered to read Charles's *Mother Earth News* article published the year before, they would have seen his stated intent in moving to the Trion property was to "get back to basics…be poor!" But alas, they did not.

Chapter 7
THE CRIMES

In early December, both West and Brock participated in a Bible study at West's sister's house on the importance of the family unit. On Sunday, December 12, 1982, just two days after this discussion on the value of the love of Christ, the two men decided to put their plan into action. A weapon in hand seemed like a good idea, so the seventeen-year-old asked to borrow his mother Betty Jo Lowrance's .22-caliber rifle. He used the same reason he'd given her numerous times before: he was going rabbit hunting. The two went over to West's sister Myra Haygood's trailer to watch some football for a while that afternoon with Myra's nineteen-year-old son, Joey Lavon Wells.

Wells had met Teresa Hudgins for the first time earlier in the day, when he was out with Brock, whom Hudgins had known for three years. Hudgins had been dating James Lamar Blevins for a few weeks but had accepted a date with Wells that day when the attractive young man asked her out. He told her that his car was not working so his mother would come pick her up. In fact, however, his trial testimony revealed that Wells's dad was at the time withholding the keys to Wells's car. So Myra went to Blevins's home, where Hudgins and her daughter had been staying, to fetch her son's date for the night. Hudgins told Blevins she was just going to play bingo in Rome. Instead, the two women went back to Myra's trailer around 6:00 p.m. West and Brock apparently thought it would be good cover to have the adolescents along with them. At one point, West tried to claim it was Wells who asked that he and Hudgins be allowed to come along with him and Brock, but West also later said that he thought their presence would keep Charlie from trying any "homosexual stuff," so they invited Wells and Hudgins to come riding around. Many people have speculated over the years about Joey Wells's role that night. Did he know the plan ahead of time? Brock claimed Wells had helped plan the evening's events. Wells has always denied it, though Hudgins's trial testimony that Wells took some items for himself leaves some doubt about that denial. However, without a doubt, Teresa Hudgins had no idea what was about to happen.

The four climbed into West's ten-year-old Javelin with West driving, Brock next to him and Wells and Hudgins in the back. Not wanting to run out of gas, they stopped at the Red Barn convenience store and sent the young couple in to get a dollar's worth of gas and a pack of Marlboro cigarettes. When they came back out, Brock told them they were going "on top of the mountain to the devil worshipper's house." Hudgins responded, "Who and what is devil worshippers?!" Brock reassured her, telling her they were just a couple of gay men who had homemade wine. (All quotes in this chapter are taken directly from the *State v. Tony West* trial transcript.) On the way there, everyone started huffing a noxious mix of paint thinner, glue and alcohol known as toot-a-loo. As Hudgins put it in her trial testimony, during which she acknowledged huffing the toot-a-loo herself that night two or three times, they did it in the car "all the way [to] on top of the mountain." Those who could afford it might snort cocaine, but the ingredients for toot-a-loo could be purchased cheap at the local hardware store and mixed up in a bleach bucket.

Up the mountain they went. When they arrived, as was his habit, Dr. Scudder came out to greet them and asked for a cigarette for Joey, who was still in the kitchen. Scudder invited them up to the Pink Room, so they all scaled the outside ladder to the third floor of the Chicken House, Brock carrying the toot-a-loo bucket. As it was a cold night, Scudder turned on the kerosene heater and lit a lantern and then reclined on the mattress where Brock and West were sitting. He turned to Wells and Hudgins, who were on another mattress, and asked their names, as he had never met the couple. West admired a medallion around the professor's neck, lifting it from his chest to get a better look at it and questioning Charles about it. Brock asked for more wine, so Charles went to fetch it. According to Wells, West and Brock were both drinking from the same flask as Dr. Scudder, whereas he and Hudgins had their own flask, though West would contend at trial that the professor had his own flask. After Charles returned, Brock left under the pretense of getting more toot-a-loo, ignoring Wells's worried attempt to stop him. He got the rifle from the car and returned to the Pink Room. Scudder, a bit tipsy in his playroom, didn't respond with fear but instead laughed and said, "Bang bang."

One thing Charles Scudder's associates in both Chicago and Georgia agreed on was the professor's uncanny, almost hypnotic ability to persuade anyone to do whatever he wanted. As one friend put it, "He could talk you into anything or out of it." His sexual exploits both in person and on paper with his partner's apparent blessing were proof of that, as was the fact that, although locals had shown up on more than one occasion with the intent to cause trouble for the pair they considered an abomination, Charlie had always managed to persuade them to leave without getting so much as a scratch. He had a keen sense of what motivated people and how to mollify them. So perhaps he realized Brock's intent but thought he could defuse it, as he had with others.

It worked for a while. Brock laughed, laid down the gun and sat again with West and the professor. They chatted and drank for perhaps another twenty minutes. But when Charles rose again to trim the lamp, Brock grabbed him by the hair and pulled his head back while putting a knife to his throat. Charles, perhaps pretending, continued to treat it as a laugh. "What kind of game do you want to play? I'll play your game." In response, his attacker hurled him on the mattress and tied his arms behind his back with strips of sheet he cut up and passed through holes he slashed in the sleeves of Dr. Scudder's thick coat. The enraged Brock demanded to know where the money was, and Charlie honestly responded he did not have any, as his money was, after all, in the bank. His assailant's response was to cut more strips to bind him further. According to both Joey Wells's testimony and Hudgins's statements to Pam Purcell, at this point Hudgins was nearly beside herself with panic. Tears streamed down her cheeks as she pleaded, "Don't hurt nobody. Let us go!" Still the concerned host, Charlie managed to ask before he was gagged if she was all right. Her disbelieving response was, "You'd better worry about yourself!"

Not wanting any part in what was about to happen, Teresa Hudgins and Joey Wells bolted down the ladder. West followed with the gun and ordered them to return, claiming he didn't want to hurt anyone but would if he had to. Wells cajoled West into the car instead, but the engine wouldn't start. West took it as a sign that the evening's events were "meant to happen." Defeated, they returned with him to the Pink Room.

The two killers continued to demand the location of the money. Having forgotten to bring their own, they asked Charles if he had a soldering iron. Throughout it all, Charles maintained his almost preternatural calm. During this time, Joey Odom was clearing away the kitchen in the manor, unaware of the nefarious events unfolding nearby. It occurred to the diabolical duo that they might have better luck with him. West tossed the gun to Brock, who disappeared down the hatch with it. As soon as he was out of earshot, Joey Wells took the opportunity to beg his uncle to abandon the plan: "You don't need this on you. Let's just get out of here." West took a resigned approach, responding, "It's a way of life." Brock, meanwhile, loudly commanded Odom to "get the dogs and come out of the house!" The four remaining in the Chicken House suddenly heard a barrage of bullets. Brock returned a few minutes later, announcing, "I killed that man and those dogs." He later claimed that he fired because Joey had reached for his own gun when he saw the rifle in his hand. However, nothing in the trial record indicates that Joey had a gun within reach. The predators then dragged the professor, still bound, down the ladder and into the kitchen, where he was forced to witness the evil inflicted by these two he had invited into his home. Joey Odom lay on the floor with four bullet holes in his head and one in his arm, his blood melting thickly across the floor like warm molasses. To those present, he appeared dead, though there was some dispute in court later about whether he had, in fact, already expired at this point. Brock had also shot the two huge dogs, which had strangely remained curled around a wood heater in the room during the murder of their master rather than attacking to defend him. According to Brock, the shots were all fired in one continuous volley, which could explain their behavior. Tony West would later shoot the already dead dogs again. Upon seeing his beloved partner sprawled in the huge crimson pool, Charles cried out through his gag. Up until hearing the shots, it had not truly sunk in for him that his lifestyle of wild abandon had not just put him at risk—it had claimed the life of the only other person he truly loved. Some speculate that Charles gave up the idea of living at this point.

West forced Charles past the body and into the library, where he pushed the gag up momentarily to allow his hostage to answer his continuing demands for money and requests for a soldering iron. Charles, despondent over the death of his companion, pointed out that he had no electricity and, therefore, no soldering iron. His feet still bound, Charles tried to make his way back to minister to his lover. He ignored Tony's warning, "Sit back down or I'll shoot you," responding cryptically, "I asked for this." This comment has been the source of much speculation over the years. Was he referring to his dangerous lifestyle? To their habit of welcoming total strangers into their home? Had he at last awakened a dragon too dangerous to handle? Or was this a reference to dabbling recklessly with the occult? Mark Fults believes

The dogs were shot where they lay, curled around a stove. *Bobby Gilliland.*

his comment referred to inviting evil into his home, similar to the old myths and stories about vampires being able to enter a house only upon invitation. Once one willingly brings evil in, he may not be able to control it. This belief is prevalent among pagans and Christians alike and certainly describes what happened when Charles brought the murderous pair into their home that fateful night.

True to his word, when Charles continued to struggle toward Joey, West shot him in the face. The first shot brought him to his knees but didn't kill him, so as he tried to struggle to his feet, West pulled the trigger again and again, knocking him into a sitting position in front of the library bookcase. When all was said and done, Tony West had fired four rifle rounds into the professor's head. He appeared dead, leaning against the bookcase, eyes glazed.

Brock, in the meantime, was crowing about how rich they were going to be. He was running wildly up and down the stairs, tossing the house, looking for the money for which they had killed. The ruthless robbers were to be disappointed. They found a few coins, a little jewelry, a leather jacket,

The professor's body as found by law enforcement, with pink gag and hands tied. Two flasks of his potent homemade wine can be seen on the couch. *Bobby Gilliland.*

a pair of handcuffs, more flasks of wine, a gold-plated dagger with a jewel-encrusted handle, some silver candelabras and a pistol that Brock pocketed. There were items of great value in the home, but the heavy sixteenth-century furniture could neither be moved nor carried, and the thought of taking the macabre Mephistopheles statue and other Satanic artwork from the home of the two souls they had just exterminated was likely too unnerving for this provincial pair. As the Javelin had not started earlier, the killers decided to take the victims' vehicle, and the gold-plated harp would not fit in the Jeep by their estimation. They missed the three vials of LSD-25 in a box in the bottom desk drawer.

Teresa Hudgins did not participate in the ransacking. West forced Joey Wells up the stairs to help Brock so that the older man could "talk to Teresa." This turned out to be just an excuse to get the terrified teen alone in order to proposition her. As with the initial planning, there is some dispute about Wells's participation in looting the house. He denies taking part and says he and Hudgins only loaded the items into the dead couple's Jeep because they were ordered to by Brock and West. Hudgins claimed that Wells actually took some items himself. When Brock proposed burning down the home to destroy the evidence, it was Wells who pointed out the fire would draw attention. The idea, according to Wells, was abandoned (though someone in the crime scene investigation video can be heard observing that you could see where they tried to pour gasoline on the floor to burn the place and bodies up but couldn't get it lit). Fortunately for Hudgins, her date did not remain upstairs long.

When Wells and Brock came back into the library, Brock shoved Charles's limp body sideways so that he could get at the drawer in the bookshelves behind him. A short while later, strangled sounds came from the professor. Brock had had enough. He stood over Charles with the pistol he had found upstairs and fired the fifth shot in the center of his forehead, crowing that he had gotten him "right between the eyes." The professor lay there gagged, blood everywhere, while his killer bragged, "Now by God tell me I don't have the guts to kill somebody." As they continued searching the home, to their astonishment, the men heard Joey Odom making gurgling noises. Though they all thought he was dead, he had managed to drag himself from his original position halfway between the kitchen and the dining area all the way into the latter. Brock, still carrying the pistol, went into the dining room, and another shot rang out. He had used Charles's own .22-caliber revolver to finish off the man's beloved companion.*

Finally, the Jeep was loaded. They did not notice, as they exited, the painted, half-closed eyes of Charles Scudder staring down at them from the prescient self-portrait he had executed before his death. Friends report that it was actually Joey who had the vision depicted in the portrait in the middle of the night, sometime after his wreck. After he described it to his partner, Charlie got up and painted it. The painting was both eerily uncanny and terrifying in its clairvoyance.

---

* There has been much debate and disagreement about who shot who with which gun, in which order and how many shots were fired. From the very beginning and continuing through both the criminal and property cases, both eyewitnesses gave multiple accounts that differed from each other and even their own earlier versions, and these descriptions varied from those given by the killers. Given the stress they were under that night and the multiple horrors inflicted, it is not surprising that Teresa Hudgins and Joey Wells should not remember exactly all the details of the shots, especially given that they each acknowledged averting their eyes for most of the gunfire. However, the physical and medical evidence is this: Medical examiner Dr. James Dawson found that, though there were five bullet holes in Scudder's head, only four bullets were recovered, and they all came from a rifle. Dr. Dawson speculated that the fifth bullet passed through and was never recovered. Both eyewitnesses testified that Kenneth used the rifle on Odom, Tony used the rifle on Charles and Kenneth fired the final shot or shots into Charles's head with a pistol. The testimony varied about whether or not Odom was shot with the pistol. The only pistol shot that was recovered came from Joey Odom's skull, along with four rifle slugs from his head and one shot to his arm. This, therefore, is the only rational explanation that reconciles all those facts.

Charles Scudder's eerily prescient self-portrait depicting himself just as he was found: gagged with five bullet holes in his head. *Courtesy Ralph Van Pelt.*

It depicted Charles, gagged, with five bullet holes in his forehead.

Candice Williamson confirmed that Charles said it was a self-portrait, and another friend of the couple's, Tracey Wilson, said that Charles had told her about the painting, "That's how I'm going to die."

Brock left in the loaded Jeep. West managed to get his Javelin to finally start, and he departed in that, after putting Joey Wells and Hudgins in the back. They returned to the older man's trailer, where he vowed retribution if Wells or Hudgins called the law. He said he and Brock were heading for the Philippines and would send for the two young people later. Finally, after being reminded by Brock to remove Charles's leather jacket first, West walked them back to his sister's trailer. When she was finally alone with her date, Hudgins declared that she wanted to call the police. Wells told her they weren't calling the law, as "I'm not going to get my uncle into trouble." He told her she had to stay with him "until things cooled off." Anxious to get rid of the Javelin, West sold it to Wells and his mom for seven dollars, which was all they had between them, and the promise to send another sixty-eight dollars later. Myra Haygood, Wells's mother, started to take Hudgins home, asking, "What's wrong?" after noticing the couple was behaving strangely. Hudgins dissolved into tears and told Myra the whole story along the way. Myra reiterated Wells's command not to call the police. She took the distraught young woman around midnight back to James Blevins's home to pick up Hudgins's little girl. Unknown to Myra, Hudgins pulled Blevins aside in the back room and told him she had witnessed two murders that evening before Myra led her back to the car and returned with Wells and her two-year-old daughter to her trailer. Knowing she would likely not heed their warnings, they kept Hudgins there with no access to a phone for four days before she finally managed to call her uncle on December 16, when Wells took her to a friend's house to play cards.

West and Brock had told their families they were going to Florida but instead headed west in the Jeep through Alabama and Mississippi, talking vaguely about possibly heading to Mexico. They pulled into a rest stop east of Vicksburg, Mississippi, late on the night of December 13 to sleep and regroup. An off-duty highway patrol officer actually spotted them there, but as they had not yet been identified as suspects, he thought nothing of the vehicle with its unusual markings and went on his way. The fugitives had already discussed ditching the Jeep for something less conspicuous and, according to Bobby Gilliland, had been thinking about trying to find a Toyota, so when they woke up and saw Lieutenant Kirby Key Phelps alone and sleeping in a Toyota next to them, it was as if someone had answered their prayers. West snatched up the revolver while Brock reached for the handcuffs. When West pointed the gun directly at him, the startled Phelps responded, "Take anything you want, just don't shoot me!" He allowed himself to be cuffed and stumbled through the woods and over a fence with West at his side, while Brock transferred their belongings and Charles's to the Toyota. West attempted to cuff Phelps to a pine tree but had to unlock the left cuff to do so, and when he did, Phelps threw a right-handed punch at him. West immediately shot him three times in the head, took his wallet and identification and left him in the woods while he escaped in the dead man's car. In the meantime, Brock drove the Jeep to the other side of Vicksburg and into Louisiana, then abandoned it and rejoined West. West had removed the license plate from the Javelin when he sold it to Joey Wells and his mother. The tag actually belonged to West's mother, Nelda West. At some point, the assassins thought to switch it out with the license plate on the Toyota. The murderers fled through Louisiana and Texas on their path toward Mexico. By the time a Civil War relic hunter discovered the unidentified body of Kirby Phelps early on December 15, they were long gone.

Chapter 8

THE DISCOVERY

Back in Chattooga County on the day Phelps's body was discovered, Raymond Williams decided to drop by Corpsewood to tell the twosome that a mutual friend, Roy Hood, had died in Rome the day before. Raymond had visited the pair—in fact, on the last day of their lives—to convey that Roy was in the hospital. He brought along his recorder and made an audiotape of Charles playing a haunting melody on his harp while reciting lines from William Blake's poem "The Tyger." None of the three had any idea that in less than eight hours, the couple would be lying in pools of blood mere feet from each other, eyes glazed over, never to see again. Raymond followed the rising Mountain View Road until the pavement ran out and then continued up the dirt road into the woods, going right at the first turnoff and traveling until he finally reached their driveway, Dead Horse Road, on the left. When he reached the manor, he did not see their Jeep. Assuming it was Grocery Day, he left without approaching the door. The shattered glass thus went unnoticed, and another day passed with the killers unpursued. The next morning would tell a different tale, however.

Upon seeing that the car was still gone when he arrived the next morning, Williams felt the light touch of the first fingers of unease. As he approached the utility door yawning open, revealing the bullet-riddled kitchen door, that gentle tickle transformed to the raking nails of alarm. In these days before cellphones, he jumped in his car and sped down Taylor's Ridge to Mountain View to call the police.

The Chattooga County Sheriff's Office was located in downtown Summerville. Even though they had been to the area near Corpsewood before, it took Deputies Charles Starkey and Greg Latta several minutes to traverse the mountain roads and dirt paths. When the deputies saw the entrance that had alarmed Williams, they knew they would find nothing good within. Two things struck them as they entered the house: the stench of filth and death and, in the small space of the house, the sight of Scudder, Odom and the two dogs lying on the floor. Greg was in front, so when he spotted and commented on the big dogs, Starkey's alarm kicked up a notch. He, like many others, had heard that the dogs were lethal killing machines. He pulled his pistol, but even after determining they were no longer a threat, he remained on guard, not knowing whether a killer still lurked in the shadowy spaces of this darkest of castles.

They proceeded to search the house for other victims or perpetrators and then called Sheriff Gary McConnell to report what they had found. The sheriff and his chief investigator, Tony Gilleland, hastened to the scene. They examined the house as well and then called in the Georgia Bureau of Investigation (GBI), FBI

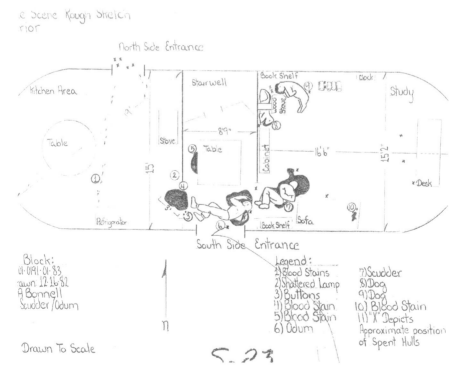

An investigator's diagram of Corpsewood. *Brad Bonnell, Tony West court file.*

and the GBI's State Crime Lab. The FBI declined jurisdiction, as the proximity to the national forest was not sufficient to bring the case within its purview, but the others dispatched their people promptly. The parade to Corpsewood, which would continue for days in soaring numbers, had begun.

Luck having sat silently on the sidelines for four days, Serendipity saw fit to intervene. On the day his body was found, Dr. Scudder's Jeep was also at last discovered where it had been abandoned in Tallulah, Louisiana, and was quickly connected to the professor. Louisiana officials called the Chattooga County Sheriff's Office about Dr. Scudder even as the sheriff himself was searching Scudder's property. McConnell jumped into action as soon as he got the message about the Jeep. Once he returned the call and informed officials there about the crime scene at the residence of the Jeep's owner, things began to fall into place. Some .22-caliber bullets had been found in the vehicle, and the highway patrol officer had disclosed seeing the unusual Jeep at the place Kirby Phelps's body was found. The location and identification of the automobile at last eradicated the fog shrouding the case, revealing the ties between the murders. But they still did not have a suspect. Nor did they have a clear picture of what had happened at the castle.

The officers searching the house, reeling from the discovery of one after another of Corpsewood's darkly bizarre secrets, were taxed with the task of putting it all together in a way that made the murders make sense. And yet the abundance of the aberrant and extraordinary overwhelmed their senses and gave free rein instead to the imaginations they usually kept under control. As they entered the house, a fetid wall of miasma struck them. Many of these men were used to the smell of death, but the odor in Corpsewood went beyond that. The sickening perfume of rotting bodies combined with the unwashed reek of body odor, the taint of spoiling food and the general effluvia of filth. So strong was the stench that every single person who was at the scene that day still recalled and brought up the smell when they were interviewed thirty-three years later. In fact, when Dove Broadcasting made the documentary *Corpsewood* beginning a few months after the murders, not only did the narrator comment on the smell that still lingered, but you could actually see in the film the thick cloud of flies that blanketed the land after the murders. Curiously, Candice Williamson does not recall such a stench in the home during the couple's lifetime, and none of those who encountered them in life made note of any hygienic issues, but in death, both they and their home had become redolent with the pungent bouquet of decay, dross and the rank and gamy aroma of stale male musk.

Inside the door was a bucket of water containing a drowned rat. Investigators wondered if this was the simple accident of a creature so stupid it would

The nasty stove, pots and pans and heavily stained flyswatter hanging with the kitchen implements contributed their share to the odor of Corpsewood. *Courtesy Ralph Van Pelt.*

intentionally climb up a bucket and jump to its death or if it was something more sinister, perhaps a setup for some sort of spell. The water in the pond was also nasty. Completely aside from the blood and other noxious substances associated with the murder, the couple themselves were dirty, unwashed and unkempt. Scudder even had a yellowed toenail that extended nearly an inch past his toe.

Once they got past the smell, the contents of the manor and Chicken House inundated the investigators anew. The whips, the chains, the handcuffs, the Satanic art, the black candles everywhere, the pornography, the endless graphically sexual letters from prisoners and other men—all unnerved them. When they discovered the skulls scattered around the house, their original thoughts were that these were yet more remains of murder victims, perhaps murdered by the latest victims. Some of the skulls were replicas, but two—one found by the desk and a more worn one on the clock—were actual human skulls. These skulls were identified as having come from Loyola, as according to Bobby Gilliland, they had characteristics of skulls that came from the same region from which Loyola got its anatomical skulls. Bobby actually had an encounter of the entirely too-close kind with one of the skulls. In those days, not only was smoking allowed in public buildings, but it

This drowned rat was discovered in a pail of water in the area with the cleaning supplies. *Courtesy Ralph Van Pelt.*

The woefully low pond during the criminal investigation. Zeke Woodall later paved it with floor mats. *Bobby Gilliland.*

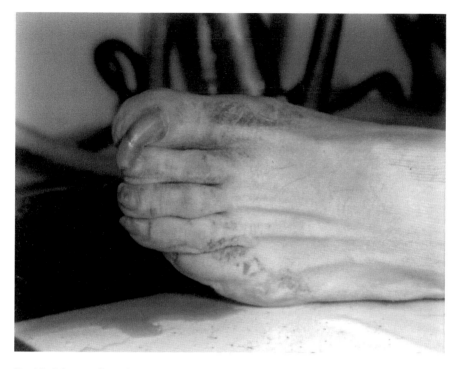

Scudder's long, yellowed toenail. *Courtesy Ralph Van Pelt.*

was not uncommon to see investigators smoking during the examination of the crime scene itself, and this stupefying scene was certainly no exception. Bobby was smoking as he examined the professor's library and stretched his hand out to tip his ashes into what he thought was an ashtray on Scudder's desk when one of the other officers yelled, "What are you doing??" The item he had almost desecrated with his cigarette was actually one of the human skulls! (These skulls were not as unique a souvenir as one might think. One of the family members suing for "desecration of a corpse" in the crematory case displayed a relative's skull on a bookshelf.)

The unease stirred by the skulls was aggravated by the discovery of excavation in the yard. The officers thought they were seeing newly dug graves. They arranged to have the area dug up the next day with the help of—what else?—prison trustees. Though the digging eventually proved to be innocent, at the time the investigators did not know what to think, what with bodies, skulls, apparent graves, Satanic and other occult items and all the sadomasochistic paraphernalia and other sexual material. What sort of hell had they wandered into?

Dr. Scudder had several skulls, including two human ones: one by his desk and one on the clock. *Bobby Gilliland and Tony West court file.*

As the day wore on, the lawmen concluded that flashlights would soon be no match for the gloom of the unlit manor, so they brought in a generator and strung up electric bulbs to dispel the oncoming night. At last, the bodies of both man and beast were bagged and put in the back of the pickup truck that would serve as a hearse for the short trip to the Summerville funeral home where the autopsies would be performed. The removal of the bodies did nothing to end the traffic to the crime scene, however; reports of the nightmarish situation had gone out over the police radio and been picked up by the media, and word quickly spread to the general public as well. The human hunger for the strange and grotesque drove hundreds to follow the path up the mountain and down the gravel road in an attempt to catch a glimpse of the misery within or perhaps even acquire a souvenir or two. Many would come to regret the latter. Sheriff Gary McConnell may not have been able to eliminate the parade of gawking gossips, but he was able to establish a line where "the buck stops here."

Chapter 9

THE SHERIFF

G ary McConnell was the youngest Georgia sheriff in recent history and, at six feet, five inches, one of the largest and most physically imposing sheriffs the area has ever had. He had become a deputy shortly after graduating high school when his father was elected sheriff in 1965 and was appointed to fill his unfinished term when John Frank McConnell died in 1967. He was subsequently elected and quickly became one of the most popular sheriffs Northwest Georgia has seen. He was highly intelligent and had an abundance of political acumen, enormous charisma and a great deal of common sense. His methods were effective, even if they might have outraged big city cops who would not dream of ignoring the minnows slipping through the net in order to lure the lurking shark. The small-time moonshiners for which the county was famous may have occasionally been overlooked, but Gary McConnell's overriding concern was the safety of his jurisdiction from dangerous criminals, and the bootleggers proved at times to be excellent confidential informants. He kept his finger on the pulse of the area, and many people will still tell you today that nothing ever happened in Chattooga County without Sheriff McConnell knowing about it. Even if he could not prove that a particular individual was behind nefarious events, he found a way to make sure they stopped. At one time, a stranger appeared in town and began stopping young girls as they got off the school bus, asking if he could take their photos. Unsettled parents complained to the sheriff's office. Sources report the sizable sheriff conveyed the possible consequences of

Gary McConnell on the right, with Tony Gilleland, Earl McConnell, Eddie Lumpston and Greg Latta. The metal door at right lies there still. *Bobby Gilliland.*

his actions to the alleged photographer. Whatever he said must have made an impact—the fellow never troubled the daughters of the area again.

Not everyone viewed Sheriff McConnell in such a favorable light, however. Grumblings in Chattooga County mention the "Dixie Mafia" and complain of corruption. These grumblings generally originated among those who had themselves or whose loved ones had been charged "unfairly," according to them. The most publicized opponent of the sheriff was County Commissioner Harry Powell. The commissioner and sheriff had a long-standing feud. One source said that it originated in a real estate dispute. So when the sheriff, along with then-district attorney Earl Self, brought felony charges against Powell for allegedly sodomizing prisoners, the commissioner immediately cried "Foul!" The trial ended in a victory for Powell on August 29, 1975, when the jury acquitted him after just an hour of deliberation. The animosity between the two powerful political foes, however, was not characteristic of the sheriff's relationships.

Gary maintained a good relationship with the attorneys in the area. While he had no time for green attorneys who did not know what they were doing, skilled lawyers would occasionally have a chat with the sheriff to find out if there was something their client was not telling them, which might be important in the decision on whether to plead or go to trial. The attorneys' amiable connection with the sheriff's office did not, however, necessarily extend to other law enforcement agencies. A few years after the Corpsewood case, the GBI would target attorneys and even judges and their family in the area with "Operation Sand Doom," where they spent plenty of taxpayer money to set up a dummy company, Just Jeans, Inc., for two years, with the purpose, according to some lawyers in the area, of taking out legal personnel who were thorns in their side. Only two members of the legal community and three other people were eventually arrested (one mid-trial), but it did nothing to improve relations between the two sides. The sheriff's office, however, was not a party to this animosity in the small-town legal community. Gary McConnell was a big man with a big future, and he knew the importance of maintaining civil relationships with influential individuals.

Eventually, Gary would impress Georgia governor Zell Miller by freezing all the crazed traffic on a congested New York City street in order for the governor to cross, while the stunned drivers looked on, slack-jawed. Miller later appointed him the head of Emergency Management. He knew that a man with enough presence, authority and get-'er-done attitude to stop New York traffic could handle that job. Later, when he was promoted to head of the State Olympic Law Enforcement Command, he dealt with the massive security headaches surrounding Atlanta's 1996 Olympics.

The massacre was not Sheriff McConnell's first encounter with Corpsewood. Rumors of deviant sex and Satanist celebrations had reached the county's chief law enforcement officer years before, and they didn't sit well with the protector of God-fearing Chattooga County. At this point, Georgia had a law on the books making all kinds of sodomy illegal, but it was the prospect of Black Masses being performed in Trion that really disturbed the residents. As he revealed to reporters in a press statement, "It was pretty well known they were devil worshippers. We looked into prosecuting them, but there was nothing we could do—that's just freedom of religion."

His immediate concern now was the protection of the crime scene. Gary knew the propensity of people to collect "souvenirs" from gruesome cases. He knew he couldn't keep the curious off the mountain. What he *could* do, however, was set up a roadblock at the end of Dead Horse Road so ghouls looking for a thrill could go only so far and no farther. Not that that kept everyone completely out. When the media got hold of a story that included devil worship, a hand-built castle in the middle of the woods, sexual deviance, exotic drugs and murder, they had a field day. The story spread rapidly first through the country and then the world. Network news stations, international tabloids, local and national newspapers—all wanted a piece of the story. It wasn't long before one of the television stations thought to hire a helicopter to get shots from above that they were not allowed to take on the ground. But McConnell knew how to distinguish between necessary mandates within his ability and those things beyond his control that would not make a difference to his case, so he let the helicopter flying overhead go. The roadblock lasted long enough for law enforcement to get everything they needed from the scene, but when the dam broke, a tidal wave of humanity came pouring into the property. A constant stream of the curious came to gape at the extraordinary estate of the two eccentrics. A group of ministers took their own private tour of all the buildings. Someone left crosses on the property. Fistfights broke out between friends of the couple and souvenir-seekers. Rosebushes were ripped out, to be replanted at the homes of the thieves like trophies celebrating a triumph over evil. The masses broke open the steel castle doors that had been welded shut (one of which lies on the ground there to this day), and the manor itself was invaded by the probing public, its private secrets paraded in a very public display without so much as a fig leaf to cover its exposed intimate details.

When he got the call about the Jeep, Gary McConnell finally had his first break in the case. Though he knew the murder in Mississippi and the Jeep in Louisiana were somehow connected with the murders in his county, he was still not sure how. They initially thought, after reading through the dozens of sexually charged letters from all over the country, that the murderer must be one of the convicts with whom Scudder corresponded. The fact was, they needed another, much bigger break. And Providence was about to drop it in their laps, in the form of one Teresa Hudgins.

On December 16, Hudgins had managed to call her family to tell them what had happened. They told her that if she wanted to avoid having to go to jail herself, she had better go to the police right away. So after finally getting away from Wells when friends came to pick her up on Thursday, she went to her parents' home on Lyerly Street in Summerville and called the sheriff around nine o'clock the following night. Gary was out investigating the Corpsewood murders, but she impressed on the sheriff's office the importance of her call. They managed to get the message to him fairly quickly, and he returned the call within the hour. Hudgins told him solemnly that she had information about the "devil worshipper killings" and told him to come by himself. When he finally arrived, the Hudginses had managed to round up Joey Wells and his mother. Recognizing that Hudgins, not Wells, was the one who had called him, Gary didn't waste any time and took her statement on the spot. She purged herself of the pent-up demons of that night for forty-five minutes, after which Gary took both teens to the sheriff's office, where they would each talk for several hours more. At 2:30 a.m., murder warrants were issued for West and Brock. GBI agents were dispatched to Brock's mother's trailer, where they seized the Remington .22 automatic rifle that had been used to kill Scudder and Odom.

Meanwhile, West and Brock were still in Texas, never having made it to Mexico. They had been on the run for days, they were running out of money and they were fighting about everything. West still wanted to go to Mexico; Brock did not. West later claimed Brock seemed to want to kill someone else while he did not. On Saturday, December 18, they decided to go to a topless bar to cool off, but the women and the alcohol and the atmosphere did not help anything. Their nerves frazzled to the breaking point, West growled at the younger man to get lost. Brock did not need to be told twice. He hitched his way back to Georgia. Ironically, one of the men who gave him a ride was an off-duty police officer who had no idea that the youth in his car was wanted for three murders. A week and a day after the massacre at Corpsewood, Brock called Betty Jo Lowrance from a gas station in Marietta, Georgia. She told him about the charges, and he told her it was West and not him who had done the killing. He asked her to come pick him up. On a hunch (which Brock would claim was based on an illegal wiretap), Chattooga County Sheriff's Office investigators Tony Gilleland and Ron Turner stopped by the Lowrance trailer that same evening and quickly got the truth out of Betty Jo. Down in Marietta, having finally opened the floodgates on his emotions, Brock couldn't seem to close them. While waiting for his mother, he told the gas station employees that he was wanted for murder in Summerville. Gary and his deputies, not wanting the young man to take off again, requested law enforcement in the area to take him into custody. He was arrested at 6:30 p.m. His subsequent confession sparked the sheriff to request the U.S. Navy have someone try to identify the as yet unknown Mississippi body, as Brock had told them about the navy identification card they removed from the dead man. At last, on Tuesday, December 21, nine days after the murders of Charles Scudder and Joseph Odom, the remains from the rest stop were identified as Lieutenant Kirby Key Phelps.

Perhaps fearing that Brock would be caught and confess, as indeed happened, West changed his destination from Mexico to Oklahoma. He made it as far as Missouri and then turned and headed back to Chattanooga. Much to his surprise, the stress, loneliness and isolation, particularly during the holidays, was even crueler than the possible prospect of prison. He arrived in Chattanooga on Christmas Eve. The termination of the trip was filled with the same mixture of misfortune and malevolently perverted luck that had characterized the entire horrific sequence of events. He ran out of gas on Rossville Boulevard a short distance from the Georgia line. Disgusted, he decided to walk to the nearby Palomino Club Lounge, in the process getting soaked to the bone by the rain coming down in great sheets. The deluge saturated every thread of his clothes—clothes that bore the label of Kirby Key Phelps. It must have seemed like a sign from God when, after finally arriving at the club, who should he run into in the parking lot but Chattanooga police officer Gene Haas? Certain he was about to be arrested, and too exhausted to run farther, West approached him with his hands outthrust for the cuffs, saying, "Go ahead and take me in." Haas had no idea what he was talking about. "What for?" he responded. West told him he had killed some people in Summerville. Apparently, the news that had been 'round the world had not made it to all the members of the Chattanooga Police Department, so Haas ran a National Crime Information Center (NCIC) report on West twice. Miraculously, he got no hits either time, so, clearly puzzled by West's assertions but sympathetic to the dripping wet man's plight, he offered to give him a ride across the line to Rossville, Georgia, after assuring him there were no outstanding warrants for him. He took him to the Rossville Police Department, where someone thought to call officers in Chattooga County. In a twisted take on the constant conflict over truth between law enforcement and criminals, only after Chattooga adamantly confirmed the existence of the warrants did the officer at last believe Tony West's assertions that he should be arrested for murder. But that was not the end of the story. The police agencies were concerned that it might cause a problem for their case that Haas, a Chattanooga, Tennessee patrolman, had driven West outside his own jurisdiction to a police department in Georgia. Therefore, in yet another singularly odd episode in a series of peculiar events, they decided to have Haas drive West across the state line yet again into Tennessee, followed by Rossville officers who remained on the Georgia side of the line, so that the gunman could walk back across the line to the waiting arms (and cuffs) of Rossville Police Department. Never had a murderer had to put so much effort into getting himself arrested.

When Chattooga officers finally arrived to seize West, they found him waiting casually in the lobby of the police station. Gary McConnell at last received custody of his second suspect in the wee hours of Christmas morning. It was time for the district attorney's office to kick into action.

Chapter 10

THE PROSECUTION

In 1982, David "Red" Lomenick had been the district attorney of the Lookout Mountain Judicial Circuit for less than two years. He was an old-school country lawyer, a veritable rainbow of blazing backwoods color. He would chew tobacco in court and spit the juice in the nearest Styrofoam cup, rile up the crowd at political events by calling his opponents "the attorneys for those thugs and hoodlums" and entertain juries with such phrases as "Shot like a dog, bled like a hog, but even a whore deserves to live!" during closing arguments. He was bald with white fringe, smacked his lips in a way reminiscent of one who wears dentures and had a thick country accent that seems to be the province of some rural southern lawyers and preachers. He mixed metaphors frequently, using phrases such as "the fly on the iceberg," much to the amusement of those in the courtroom. His language gaffes were not limited to phrases he created. Red had an excellent memory for case law, in part because he enjoyed reading case reports out loud. Once when he was reading "the condition was exacerbated," he interrupted himself, saying, "Exacerbated, EXACERBATED?? What the hell are they talking about? This case ain't about SEX!!" His assistants, Ann Patterson and Roland Enloe, nearly fell on the floor laughing. Red coveted the two-way radios the police had in their cars, so Gary McConnell got him one, a move he came to regret when Red would use it simply to chat, like asking someone to call his wife to see if she needed some green beans he had found on sale. Gentle suggestions that law enforcement tools were not meant for personal use, even by law enforcers, had no effect on Red, and trying to tell him what to do

Red Lomenick during the Tony West trial. *Courtesy of the* Summerville News.

would only arouse his ire. Those who knew the right buttons to push would sometimes ignite the district attorney's temper just for fun. Solicitor Patrick Clements had nearly given Lomenick an apoplexy one April Fool's Day when he lined the path the DA would take to work with his old campaign signs from a past race against Red, beginning at his home and stretching all the way to the courthouse. As in a recent presidential race, however, these foibles of an apparent buffoon did more to endear rather than enrage the public.

Red loved to rail against the "spoor of the earth, low-down, dirty-dog scum" drug dealers and other criminals. His constituents ate it up. He wasn't elected because he was a great trial lawyer but because he gave his voters the kind of theatrics they wanted. His predecessor's poor reputation did not hurt, either. Red disliked preparing cases and usually knew his limitations, so he tried very few crimes, leaving the trial work for his assistant district attorneys. Much to those assistants' chagrin, he would occasionally decide, after not reading the file or being in the courtroom for the trial, that he wanted to examine a witness or, heaven forbid, do a closing argument. More than one person recalled the tug of war over a case file between Red and an assistant that occurred in a courthouse men's room. Those cases often did not end well. At least one such case that was a surefire conviction went down the tubes when Red took over the closing argument and berated the jury that the case turned on the testimony of Mr. Green—which might have had more impact had there actually been a witness by that name in the case. The man loved an autopsy, though, and attended them whenever possible, including those of Scudder and Odom.

Though his trial skills may have left something to be desired, Red Lomenick had good instincts when it came to personnel. He hired capable assistants who could handle the trial work and brought new programs and initiatives to the Lookout Mountain Judicial Circuit, including the area's first Child Support Recovery Unit and the Victim-Witness Assistance Program. He was proud of having brought the first computers and "yore lady assistant district attorneys" to the office. He also hired excellent staff, including administrative assistants Carolyn Cooper and Sue Brock, investigator Johnny Bass and interns McCracken Poston and Michael Giglio, who would later go on to practice law in the same building in the circuit.

Poston, in fact, would be elected to the Georgia House of Representatives three years after graduating from law school, following two years of service as an assistant district attorney for Red. His flair for the dramatic is reminiscent of F. Lee Bailey, and he would go on to handle a number of cases that garnered him national recognition, as they were featured on such shows as *Dateline NBC* and *CNN Presents*. These included the Alvin Ridley case, where he had his client cleared of the charge of murdering his wife after he allegedly held her captive for thirty years; a "sex for judgments" case where, after his client revealed the judge had propositioned her, officers planted drugs in her car; and the notorious Tri-State Crematory case. At the time of his internship, however, Poston was still in school, though his flair for capturing an audience's attention with style and wit was already evident. In law school, he boldly hung a black velvet Elvis among the presidential portraits, along with a small sign proclaiming it had been executed by Dali during his black velvet period.

On the eve of the Tony West trial, intern Poston was summoned to pick his boss up from Atlanta's Hartsfield Airport. Rather than reviewing testimony and evidence, Red had been touring California during preparations for the case. While there, he visited the Roy Rogers Museum and dropped in uninvited on the Los Angeles County district attorney's office, where he lamented in hillbilly dialect his shortage of funding and staff. Poston had agreed to pick his boss up from the redeye flight as long as he could drive Red's Lincoln for the week. As students are wont to do, young McCracken had spent the evening prior enjoying Atlanta's nightlife until the wee hours. His condition early the following morning dulled his usually sharp wit to the point he was unable to stop the onslaught of tales about the marvels of seeing Rogers's horse Trigger stuffed and displayed that spewed on for the entire trip back to the northwest corner of the state. The upcoming death penalty case was clearly not on the district attorney's mind. When he reached the office, the monologue continued with illustrations; the harried staff and assistants, struggling to prepare for the imminent start of the complicated hearings on the most publicized case in their history, were all

Ralph Van Pelt during the Tony West trial. *Courtesy of the* Summerville News.

treated to a leisurely viewing of a panoply of photos of Trigger and other wonders of the West. The district attorney even took the time to tell the grand jurors of his visit with the big-city prosecution office, adding in apparent reference to the discussion on funding, "They're even more underhanded than us!" The wide-eyed and uncomfortable reaction made clear that they had not distilled the intended meaning from the remark.

The brightest rising star among Red Lomenick's assistants was Ralph Van Pelt Jr. Ralph had just graduated from the University of Georgia Law School in the summer of 1980, and after doing court-appointed criminal defense for six months, he went to work for the district attorney's office on January 1, 1981. Not many attorneys are faced with the daunting prospect of handling a capital punishment case two years out of law school, particularly one where even certain judges had expressed the opinion that there was no way it would result in a death penalty. But Van Pelt proved to be more than qualified.

Tall, lanky and solemn, Van Pelt at first glance appeared to be the bookish type that you would expect to shy from the glaring spotlight of the courtroom. That appearance was deceiving. Ralph Van Pelt harbored a thirst to prove himself, and the Tony West trial provided the perfect vehicle for that. To this day, he credits that trial with paving the way for his election as district attorney in 1988 and later appointment by Governor Zell Miller as superior court judge in 1996.

The office did not have much time to prepare the case. The vast media attention given to the murders practically mandated that this trial be given first priority over other, older cases on the docket. Preliminary hearings were held for Kenneth Brock on January 26 and Tony West on February 3, barely a month after they were arrested. Indictments by the grand jury quickly followed within a couple of weeks. Tony West's indictments would later become the bane of the district attorney's existence, but at the time, no one on the grand jury thought anything was awry. Adolescent Kenneth Brock was offered life rather than death in exchange for his guilty plea to the murders and robbery, accepted the deal and, accompanied by his attorneys Carlton Vines and Bill Slack, entered his plea on February 15, 1983. He told the judge that he had killed Joey Odom by shooting him in the temple twice, through the front door. He denied shooting Scudder, and claimed that was all West's doing. He confirmed that they had planned the crimes before going over to Corpsewood Manor.

Kenneth Avery Brock's attorney, Carlton Vines. *Courtesy of the* Summerville News.

Many people have said that Brock attempted suicide sometime after his plea in the Georgia case, possibly while the Mississippi cases (on which he also avoided the death penalty) were pending. However, his niece says that he had actually been trying to cut off his grim reaper tattoo with a sharpened spoon handle because he believed it had come to life and was looming over his bed. He apparently has told some family or friends this was because he was still hallucinating from the LSD. However, he never made a claim during the time of trial that he had been slipped any drugs and, in fact, indicated he felt no unusual effects from the wine. LSD is a water-soluble drug with a relatively short half-life, so it generally exits the system within a few days. While there are very rare reports of flashbacks, which are not fully understood but are believed to be caused by changes to the brain when the drug was used (for example, synapses created during the drug use firing at a later date), they are generally in the nature of strong memories or visual disturbances, such as seeing an "aura" around a person or a trail after a passing car, rather than the frightening tales initially recounted years ago by those whose purpose was to discourage drug use. Thus, the hallucination he described would be inconsistent with the nature of an LSD flashback.

Kenneth Avery Brock, like Tony West, has thus far been turned down for parole and remains incarcerated at Coffee Correctional Facility. To this day, he continues to maintain that his culpability in the matter lies in having fired through the door at random, the bullets ricocheting to find their mark in Odom's brain as if by magic. His sentence on that cold winter's day was handed down by Superior Court Judge Joseph E. Loggins.

Chapter II
THE JUDGE

The Honorable Joseph E. "Bo" Loggins had sat on the bench of the Lookout Mountain Judicial Circuit Superior Courts since 1977. He had actually known one of the chief witnesses in the case, Raymond "Little Goob" Williams, in his youth; his wife, Helen, in fact, recounted the story of how they had played a prank on "Little Goob" that involved towing his car all the way from Chickamauga Battlefield to Trion. Judge Loggins had attended night law school at the Woodrow Wilson College of Law and was admitted to the bar in 1955. He is an upstanding member of the community with a conservative reputation and would likely not be amused to learn that, unknown to him, he signed off on the first gay adoption in the area around twenty years before gay marriage was legalized, when a well-liked gay man in the Ringgold community adopted his partner's niece, whom they had raised together from the time she was very young.

When asked how he wished to be remembered, he responded that he wanted people to recollect him as having been honest and fair. As to the first, no one would ever accuse the jurist of being susceptible to bribes. Helen recalled that a friend of her husband's had tried to get him to rule a certain way on a case, and he refused several times, but the friend kept persisting. When Judge Loggins finally told him, "Fine, but I'll retire the next day," because surrendering his principles would render him unfit to hold the position, his acquaintance finally realized he was serious and backed off. As to the issue of fairness, however, more than one defense lawyer scoffed at that description. Judge Bo Loggins had a reputation as a prosecutor's judge.

This portrait of the Honorable Joseph E. Loggins by Suzanne Royal presides over the main courtroom of the Chattooga County Courthouse. *Amy Petulla.*

When sentencing a criminal defendant, he was in the habit of saying, preliminary to imposing sentence, "This gives me very little pleasure." Rumor was that on the occasions that phrase was changed to "This gives me *no* pleasure," the defendant had better look out because he was about to get hammered with an even longer sentence than usual. Criminal defendants had many occasions to wish that they had committed their crimes in Chattanooga or Atlanta rather than the northwest corner of the state because overcrowding in urban jails tended to result in lighter sentences. The rural Lookout Mountain circuit had a reputation for handing down harsh sentences, particularly in cases where the defendant elected a trial over a plea. This "hard on crime" stance made Loggins wildly popular with voters.

Nor were the defendants the only ones to suffer at his hands. On one of his earliest days on the bench, the judge kept the lawyers in court until 1:00 a.m. in order to finish as many matters as possible. The wife of court reporter E. Don Towns called the courthouse more than once to check her husband's whereabouts because who would believe that an officer of the court would actually keep everyone working that late? Loggins also made no secret of the fact that he did not care for lawyers who were not part of the established circle of attorneys in the circuit. New lawyers, female lawyers (who were a novelty at that time) and lawyers from out of town had better expect to be put on the spot, warranted or not. The judge was also clever about ways to avoid reversals on questionable rulings. He would ask new lawyers who might not know any better, "I assume you have no objections to my charge?" as if it was a given, and those who were uninformed enough to accede unwittingly waived permanently some of the strongest grounds for appeal they might have. If an objection was made that he knew might be valid but that he did not want to grant, he was skilled at responding in such a way that he did not actually rule on the objection, so that the ground was not preserved for appeal. Those methods included responding with a "you can't be serious" type of question and a thunderous frown, followed by a terse, "Proceed." The intimidation often worked on less seasoned attorneys.

If, however, he was forced to rule, the ruling would still generally be in favor of the state in a criminal case if it was an issue that had a serious possibility of affecting the outcome of the trial. Judge Loggins was reversed a number of times, but the reversals never seemed to bother him. His position was, "If I'm wrong, the Court of Appeals will tell me so." After all, even if he was reversed on appeal, the defendant would likely be cowed by the original guilty verdict into entering a plea in round two. In addition, some cases, such as misdemeanors, were not likely to be appealed in any event, and some rulings requested by the defense would have overruled a long-standing practice in the circuit in such a way as to cost taxpayers considerable sums. The Lowrance "right to counsel" case is a good example.

Charles Lowrance was arrested for misdemeanor theft by receiving stolen goods. Lowrance (who was later determined to, in fact, be indigent) requested and was refused an appointed attorney on multiple occasions. At trial, Judge Loggins refused and told him they were going with the case right away, whether he had an attorney or not. It was the practice in the circuit not to appoint attorneys to defendants charged only with misdemeanors. Lowrance found an attorney during a short recess after this discussion, and his trial began twenty minutes later, though there were several other defendants with counsel in the courtroom whose cases could have been called instead. Lowrance was convicted. On behalf of the defendant, attorney David Dunn alleged on appeal that the practice of never appointing an attorney for a misdemeanor defendant caused his client to be deprived of effective assistance of counsel. The Georgia Court of Appeals agreed, and the *Fulton County Daily Report*—the paper that reported the rulings of Georgia's appeals courts—ran the story on the front page on July 24, 1987, including in the story a map of the state with only the Lookout Mountain Judicial Circuit (LMJC) colored in, crowing that the Court of Appeals had informed the circuit that Georgia's laws and the Supreme Court's rulings applied to them, too.

The judges changed their appointed counsel rules, but Judge Loggins was no more fearful of reversals on appeal than before. The judge, who took up jet skiing at the age of seventy-five because it offered the thrill of a motorcycle, put his faith in his own decisions rather than be governed by the decorum and dictates of others. Some judges are exceedingly careful to make rulings in a way that will ensure their verdicts stand. The Lookout Mountain circuit's chief judge was never hampered by those concerns. He would rule as he saw fit. The Tony West case was no exception.

At the time of this trial, the Lookout Mountain Judicial Circuit used jury commissioners to personally select the citizens to be in the groups from which juries and grand juries were chosen. Such juries were often referred to as "blue ribbon juries," as those jurors tended to be the most highly educated and upstanding citizens. For some jury commissioners, that meant choosing people whom they knew went to church or held certain moral standards. That method of grand jury conscription has since gone by the wayside, for a number of reasons. For one, today's computers are a much more efficient method to ensure that jury pool members are both random and compliant with rules regarding the requisite percentages for gender, race and the like. For another, these blue ribbon jurors were hardly the "peers" of the typical defendant. But at the time, selection by hand of grand jury pool members from people with whom the commissioners were often acquainted either personally or by reputation was the standard. Nor was this method limited to the LMJC. It was used throughout Georgia and was quite common in the South. But like the old Jim Crow laws, that did not make it right.

The jury commissioners were not, however, given complete carte blanche in choosing the panel. They were told they had to select a "fairly representative cross section of the intelligent and upright citizens of the county," according to OCGA § 15-12-40 (a) (1). When one jury commissioner was asked during the hearing if he knew what this meant, his response was, "Well, it just has to be a pretty decent guy, as far as I'm concerned, not a felon, I would think, or a convicted felon, probably would not be. And intelligent, if he has—I think if he has an IQ of 18 or more, I would consider him to be intelligent enough to serve on the jury."

In this case, 52 percent of Chattooga County citizens were women; however, only 34.3 percent of the people selected by the commissioners, from which the grand jury for this case was drawn, were women, a difference of 17.7 percent. In 1982, the U.S. Circuit Court of Appeals in Georgia reversed a murder conviction (*Machetti v. Linahan*) because that grand jury pool did not contain enough women, and that case cited a Supreme Court case (*Hernandez v. Texas*, 1954) where the disparity was only 14 percent—less than the difference in the West case. Other appeals on the same ground were in the pipeline and were expected to also lead to reversals; in fact, the reversal in the *Devier v. State* case out of neighboring Rome, Georgia, was handed down just as the West trial was beginning. The district attorney's office wanted to wait and re-indict the case with a properly populated grand jury to avoid the substantial possibility of spending a boatload of money for a trial whose conviction was predestined to be thrown out.

Judge Loggins, however, was ready for a trial. This case, which had brought so much attention to the circuit for the past couple of months, about which its citizens were so excited, was not about to go on hiatus on the eve of litigation. Chattooga County was at the moment being deprived of the attention showering the Neelley case, as Alabama was getting the first shot at putting Judith Neelley before a jury. Tony West was going to court, ready or not.

Chapter 12

THE TRIAL

The lovely courthouse in downtown Summerville was a picturesque setting for a trial that would draw national interest, with its large airy courtroom overlooked by a magnificent stained-glass window behind the judge's bench and its unusual jury room window, from which onlookers in the courtroom could observe jurors fighting (leading at times to settlements after a case had already gone to the jury). At the commencement of the West trial on February 28, 1983, the architectural grande dame had dominated downtown Summerville for seventy-three years, but she carried her age well.

The courtroom was packed with television, radio and newspaper personnel, as well as curious courthouse onlookers. Trial-watching was a favorite pastime among some Chattooga County residents. In those days before *Judge Judy* and reality television, the entertainment value of the more colorful members of the Lookout Mountain Judicial Circuit's legal community presenting their clients' tales of criminal drama and domestic bliss lost was undeniable. If you wanted comedy, misdemeanor defendants representing themselves in a jury trial could often fill the bill. In one speeding case, the attractive young woman's defense was that the male officer was not paying attention to her speed but rather her beauty. She slammed the *Encyclopedia Britannica* section on the Constitution down on her counsel table and rendered the macho policeman speechless by beginning her cross-examination with, "Mr. Persinger, are you a homosexual?" Melodrama was available as well, such as in the emotional divorce argument over the raccoon, where the wife insisted it was a pet and the husband said they

The stained glass decorating the wall behind the judge's bench at the Chattooga County Courthouse. *Amy Petulla.*

bought it to raise and skin for a cap. (With the wisdom of Solomon, Judge Jon Wood ordered that the wife receive custody of the creature during its lifetime and deliver it within twenty-four hours of its death to the husband.) One Summerville courthouse regular found himself a guest of the county when, after ADA Susan Sarratt's voice cracked on the word "fondled" due to laryngitis while she was reading a molestation indictment, he started waving his arms and yelling from the back of the courtroom, "Speak up! I can't hear ya!" But no case had ever matched the spectacle afforded by "The Devil Worshippers Murder Case." As Ben Ballenger would later put it, "It was like the circus had come to town."

The police and lawyers had been barred by court order from talking to the media, but that did not deter reporters from their coverage one bit. Every aspect of the case, from the discovery of the bodies, through the trial, continuing on to the ultimate disposition of the property was dogged by members of the fourth estate. A helicopter hired by Channel Two had touched down at Corpsewood, and its passenger emerged grinning until being informed that he was walking through the ashes of the dead that had been scattered by his chopper, at which point he scrambled quickly back aboard the safety of his ride and departed. Reporters in the courtroom hung on every word, from the preliminary hearing through the last pronouncement. DA Red Lomenick found one especially pretty reporter for Channel 3 particularly distracting; during the preliminary hearing, while GBI agent Brad Bonnell testified about the lack of all utilities, including electricity, phone, water and the like, Lomenick focused instead on the lady's legs, and as soon as Bonnell fell silent, he immediately asked, "So was there any running water or 'lectricity up there?"

Jury selection in the case took three days. Jury selection in a small town in some ways is much more in keeping with the historical "jury of one's peers," where those trying you were likely to be your neighbors and others who knew you, than the same process in a large city. Several prospective jurors were excused because they admitted they had prejudged the case. Almost all of the panel had read news about the murders. The twelve finally selected had a number of connections with the people involved in the case or had already expressed strong opinions about the issues they were supposed to judge impartially. Mrs. Smith expressed her belief that temporary insanity was a copout and shared that her husband had visited the castle after the murder to check things out and had seen and already told her about some of the evidence. Mr. Stoner acknowledged he frequently ate breakfast with one of the defense attorneys. Mr. Fuller knew all the lawyers *and* all the law enforcement. The foreman himself, Mr. Harrison, knew of the victim's alleged devil worship, lack of utilities and homosexuality and had heard about people who had visited them. The final twelve and two alternates whittled out of the original one hundred were selected not because they were the most desirable but because, as with all juries, they were the least objectionable. The presentation of evidence finally commenced on Thursday, March 3.

West was represented at trial by Clifton "Skip" Patty and Benjamin Ballenger. The pair had over eighteen years of legal experience between them, despite their youthful looks. Patty's small stature hid a brilliant legal mind. Ballenger, a native of Chattooga County whose light-colored suits contrasted sharply with the somber dark clothing of the prosecutors, provided local appeal, with his familiar manner and relaxed appearance. Though they were appointed and would ultimately receive only a small fraction of what they would have charged had they been hired on the case, they devoted hundreds of hours to saving West from Georgia's infamous "Old Sparky."

Electrocution was Georgia's only method of execution from 1924 until 2001, during which time more than four hundred prisoners were dispatched. The state had just replaced its original chair in 1980. In 1996, State Representative Doug Teper would try unsuccessfully to persuade the state to switch its method to the guillotine to preserve the condemned's remains for organ donation. But at the time of the West trial, the electric chair was the only capital option, despite the fact that right before the murders, a botched Virginia execution resulted in the condemned's head and leg catching fire. A similar incident occurred in Alabama shortly after the West trial, during which it took fourteen minutes to carry out the death sentence, and in 1984, a Georgia prisoner was re-electrocuted after struggling to breathe during the six minutes it took for his body to cool enough for doctors to officially determine that he was still alive.

The defense underwent a metamorphosis during the trial, thanks to a last-minute revelation that tossed Tony West's beleaguered attorneys a life preserver to cling to. Initially, as Ralph Van Pelt put it, the two killers' defense was essentially, "We was bewitched!" In his December 27 statement to police (only one of five total confessions the man made), West had excused his actions by saying, "All I know is they were devils, and I killed them, that's the way I feel about it." (Quotes throughout this chapter are taken from *State v. Tony West* trial transcript.) They called Tracey Bell Wilson, who had made statements that, at times, Scudder would turn red all over with a frightening, terrifying look in his eyes and that he could read your mind. West testified that the furniture in the house "glowed." One of West's witnesses, Reverend Wayne Pell, testified that "anybody that does not have the spirit of the Lord in their life is an open sepulcher for demoniac possession."

But just a couple weeks before trial, Ralph Van Pelt dropped a bombshell in their lap. While searching the scene shortly after the discovery of the bodies, officers found three vials marked LSD-25 in the bottom drawer of Charles Scudder's desk. One vial was full, one was empty and one was half full, which was indicative that the vials had been used since their arrival. Dr. Giles's testimony indicated that, when full, a vial would hold approximately four thousand doses of LSD. GBI agent Brad Bonnell had neglected to list the vials in his inventory of items seized. To make matters worse, the vials had been stuck inside a plastic bag stuffed at the bottom of a crime lab bag underneath various letters, photos and a will, and that bag was stuck behind Chief Investigator Tony Gilleland's desk, "down in the cabinet behind a typewriter." The investigator agreed that he had not produced the bag when the defense attorneys came to his office to look at evidence,

Just as West testified, Dr. Scudder's harp actually did appear to glow at times, as in this unaltered photo taken during the criminal investigation. *Bobby Gilliland.*

even though he gave them other bags of photos, clothes and jewelry. He explained that, when Brad Bonnell gave him the bag, he did not realize the powerful hallucinogenic was in there, although he acknowledged that it was "possible" that he knew that a vial of LSD had been found at the scene, that they may have discussed that and while he started to say that he was not aware of the vials, he corrected the comment to "I was not aware of the vials—of the vials being in my possession," until Van Pelt contacted him that morning. Ralph, for his part, acknowledged that he was aware of the bottles but had considered them insignificant, as he contended they were old and were found in a place "where it was obviously not being used." A desk drawer, however, is hardly an abandoned niche. Dr. Scudder had clearly not forgotten the drugs there, as he had revealed their presence to Candice Williamson. This contention was also in contrast to Tracey Wilson's testimony that she knew from visiting the victims that the LSD was kept in his desk drawer, though her testimony is somewhat suspect, given her history of mental illness and her implication in her testimony that she had consumed LSD without knowing it, despite the fact that she said she always felt in an altered state of mind after she visited. Such a contention smacks a little too much of the self-serving "but I didn't inhale" excuse.

Though no mention had been made by either defendant before of feeling as if they had been drugged or were hallucinating, by the time the trial started, Tony West's defense centered on involuntary intoxication by hallucinogenic drugs. The tale he told at trial had shades of Alice Down the Rabbit Hole that had no place in his original story. In this version, he and Brock were the victims, having been drugged against their will by these two queer men who wanted to "have homosexuality with Avery" (Brock) and him. Suddenly, he was describing how his body was there but his mind was watching that body from a distance; how he started shooting at the dogs because he thought they were fat-headed lions; how the rifle went "swoosh" instead of "bang!"; how he freaked out because everywhere he looked, he saw skulls and death. It was a much more thrilling and sympathetic tale than the one he had told the officers. It was also, in all likelihood, a complete fabrication.

After gathering in pretrial motions the direction the defense was heading, Ralph Van Pelt had sought to head it off at the pass by having the wine bottles tested for LSD. The tests came back showing that there was not, in fact, any LSD in the wine. However, Judge Loggins ruled that because they had not given enough notice to the defense of the scientific proof they wanted to submit, the state could not introduce these test results. He allowed Patty and Ballenger to hold on to the tiny lifeboat they had been tossed from their sinking ship. And they paddled that lifeboat as if their client's life depended on it. Because, in fact, it did.

Some who deny that the couple would have had drugs in the manor have pointed out that the state never had the vials themselves tested. However, the prosecution had no reason to do so, as it felt such a test could only hurt its case. The attorneys representing the defense were the ones who asked for such testing but were denied. As the defendants were indigent and the bottles were in the state's possession, West had neither the funds nor the access to the containers necessary to carry out the testing, absent a court order. The vials were clearly marked with what appeared to be official pharmaceutical labels, with a number indicating it was authorized by a federal agency. Not even the state, which was the party damaged at trial by the existence of the vials, ever seriously contended that the contents were not, in fact, LSD.

The fact that the substance was found in the manor, however, was not proof it had been slipped to the killers, and the wine bottle tests proved it had not, even though the jury would never hear that proof. Furthermore, Tony West never even hinted that he might have been drugged until after the vials were discovered.

Still, the discovery at least gave the defense a plausible argument. To further establish the LSD claim, as well as accuse the prosecution witnesses of attempting to bury evidence, Clifton Patty stated in his place on the record that he had spoken to Dr. Dunn and Mr. Wuard at the Institute for the Study of Mind, Drugs and Behavior at the Stritch Medical School of Loyola University, and they confirmed that when Dr. Scudder was there, the institute ran experiments on the effects of drugs on the mind and behavior for the military. Contrary to popular belief, Dr. Karczmar did not give testimony in the trial and was in fact out of the office when Patty attempted to contact him. Scudder's curriculum vitae was offered, showing he was not just employed by but was in fact assistant director of the institute. The defense attorneys told the jury the amount of LSD discovered at the manor could "get all of Summerville high" and raked Agent Bonnell over the coals for not revealing the presence of the substance in any manner discoverable by the defense.

The attractive, self-assured GBI agent had a habit of coolly dismissing questioned tactics or potentially troubling evidence such as the drugs in this case as "unimportant," while studiously focusing on the jury or judge rather than looking at the attorney. This infuriated many lawyers, but it had been turned against him on occasion. In one such instance, during a drug bust, the irritated agent had asked the defendant regarding his excuses, "Do I have 'dumbass' written on my forehead?!!" At trial, the defendant's attorney, Christopher Townley, unnerved Bonnell on cross by squinting at him a bit and inquiring, "Mr. Bonnell, is there something written on your forehead?" During Ballenger's withering cross in the West case, however, he maintained his composure with a straight face as he professed that he felt the vials were of no evidentiary value.

For Tony West's part, he denied Brock's assertion that the night's events had been planned in advance. Joey Wells, however, testified that West and Brock had said only a few days before that they were going to live in two devil worshippers' castle. Wells testified, furthermore, that the wine tasted fine and did not cause any unusual effects, but West's memory had large gaps when it came to anything that contradicted his story. Unhampered at trial by the little fact of the test results, West claimed not only that he committed the murders of Odom and Scudder because he was under the influence of LSD they slipped him but also alleged he was *still* under the influence of the hallucinogenic when he murdered Phelps a day and a half later. In fact, he even maintained that he was "still messed up" by the acid when he talked to the police, as explanation for possibly having told officers that they had planned to rob the men, something he now contradicted. His theft of some additional flasks of wine actually abetted him in this assertion.

He had convenient lapses in memory about the actual shootings, which he also ascribed to the hallucinogen. He slipped up, however, when asked about any research he might have done into LSD. He at first said he had never read about the drug before but then added, "Just most since I have been in here [jail], that's all." He was nearly contradicted by his co-conspirator on the issue of LSD in the wine. Ralph Van Pelt and Tony Gilleland had interviewed Brock in jail that night after Tony West testified, and Brock told them that there was no LSD in the wine, and he should know, as according to Brock, he had drank more than West. Right before he was about to testify the following day, however, Brock's attorney Carlton Vines rushed into the courtroom, having just found out his client was preparing to take the stand and, in conference, reminded him that he still had charges pending in Mississippi. Brock, therefore, invoked his Fifth Amendment right against self-incrimination and refused to answer each question posed to him, even innocuous ones like where he lived. West's defense of involuntary LSD consumption was once again spared an ignominious annihilation.

West's attorneys took full advantage of the victims' many eccentricities in order to color the jurors' opinions against them. Photos of the Satanic art, the whips and chains and sex toys and the homosexual pornography; snapshots of wild parties and men exposing themselves; sex-charged letters from numerous male convicts; and testimony that Scudder was considering opening a halfway house for prisoners or maybe a Satanic temple right there in Trion, Georgia, were all offered to poison the minds of the jury. Perhaps the sentiment "Good riddance!" would prevail and the community would return a not guilty verdict in gratitude.

West took to supplementing his trial testimony with outbursts in and out of court. Court reporter E. Don Towns stated he was afraid bullets were about to start flying from the various armed officers stationed around the courtroom when on the fourth day of testimony, West stood and cried out, "I don't want to play no more!" before bursting into sobs and incoherent speech. Court personnel knew the deputies were authorized to shoot if the defendant seemed to present a danger. He was restrained by three officers, and the trial was temporarily halted while he regained his composure. During Van Pelt's closing argument the next day, when the prosecutor rhetorically asked the jury why West didn't tell the officer about the LSD, the defendant hollered out, "They didn't ask!" He began making impromptu statements to the media when transitioning to and from the courthouse, calling on God to keep the jury from falling into traps like "these other people have."

At last, the case went to the jury on the morning of Wednesday, March 8. They were out less than two hours before returning verdicts of guilty on all counts. A member later conceded that they spent less than half an hour of that time actually deliberating on their outcome. However, their work was not yet done. As this was a death penalty case, they had to return for the sentencing portion of the trial. Tony West took the opportunity afforded by the lunch break to warn the press to find out the truth "before it happens to you or your loved ones." Evidence in the sentencing phase was brief. The testimony of a relative and a minister who said that West had attended a Bible study and evidence regarding the convicted man's prior criminal record took less than two hours. As many juries do in death penalty cases, they attempted to ask the judge when he would become eligible for parole if their verdict was life, but the judge instructed them he was not allowed to answer that. Around 6:00 p.m., the exhausted jury, which had been sequestered throughout, returned a sentence of death. After prescribing that

Chattooga County Courthouse. *Amy Petulla.*

West be put to death by electrocution between the hours of 10:00 a.m. and 2:00 p.m., Judge Loggins intoned, "May God have mercy on your soul," as he sentenced Tony West to die in the electric chair on May 2, less than two months away. West's only reaction was to calmly light a cigarette. Perhaps his demeanor was so calm because he had been told about the enormous mistake the judge had made by proceeding with the trial rather than re-indicting due to the grand jury problem.

Chapter 13

THE APPEAL AND PLEA

B y the time Tony West was sentenced to death, the lawyers in the circuit were all aware that a death penalty had been overturned in neighboring Rome due to the imbalance of the male/female ratio in the grand jury pool and that the grand jury that had indicted West also had a significant imbalance. Thus, it was no great surprise to anyone when, on February 18, 1984, slightly under a year after he was sentenced to death, the Supreme Court of the State of Georgia reversed West's conviction and ordered that he be re-indicted and retried.

Death penalty cases are far more expensive to try than ordinary murder cases, and residents of small towns crying out for the ultimate justice frequently have no idea that a single such case has the potential to put the town into debt or cause a tax increase. In this case, the expense had been incurred for naught because, at the end of the day, the conviction was thrown out. The citizens of Chattooga County were furious that approximately $79,000 of their taxpayer dollars had been wasted on a trial that was now null and void when the cost of re-indictment would have been minimal—a few dollars for the grand jury's time and a few weeks' delay. They were even more furious when they found that the potential problem and solution had been presented to the judge before the trial ever began and was rejected. And thanks to Red Lomenick and the media, they *all* found out.

In the Lookout Mountain Judicial Circuit, twice per month the court would hold civil circuit day, nicknamed "pots and pans day" by some because the day was dominated by domestic cases, with parties fighting over who would get what in their divorces. On circuit day after the West appeal decision was handed down, as they were waiting for all their divorces and other civil cases to be heard, the district attorney was publicly lamenting in his inimitable way that he had told Judge Loggins that grand jury was bad, but Loggins had said they would proceed with the case anyway. Four or five attorneys heard him making these remarks at court that day. When Red was looking to cover for himself, he had no filter on what came out of his mouth, and it never even occurred to him that publicly putting the blame on the judge might not be the most politic idea.

The newspapers had a field day. The grand jurors were so enraged, they considered refusing to re-indict. Rumor has it that it took all of Gary McConnell's considerable powers of persuasion to convince them that turning a convicted serial killer loose was not the safest way to send a message.

Having successfully gotten West's conviction reversed, Patty and Ballenger had been relieved from further representation, and Tony West was appointed new counsel for his retrial. To ensure a second conviction would stand and not get reversed for something like ineffective assistance of counsel, the judge appointed West one of the best attorneys in the circuit for his appeal: Christopher A. Townley from nearby Rossville, Georgia. Not only was the tall, commanding Townley an excellent attorney, but he was also fearless when it came to representing his clients, hired and appointed alike, and did not shy away from a defense that might upset those in power. Judge Loggins would have cause soon enough to regret this particular appointment.

When he heard about the remarks Red had made regarding his pretrial discussions with the judge about whether to proceed with the trial, knowing that there was a possible issue with the indictment, Townley filed a motion for double jeopardy that, if granted, would mean that West could not be retried and would instead walk free. His allegation was that the district attorney and the judge had colluded to give the prosecution a trial run at discovering what the defense would be. They had now already heard the theories and the surprises and would be ready for them in round two.

It was Loggins's turn to be furious. He threatened to hire Bobby Lee Cook, one of the preeminent attorneys of the Southeast and a close friend of the judge, to sue the defense attorney and talked about filing a contempt action against Townley to put him in jail. For his part, Townley's attitude was that he could not simply ignore the fact that the district attorney had publicly described the ex parte conversation he had had with the judge outside of defense counsel's presence on how to proceed when this was a death penalty case with a man's life at stake. He began gathering affidavits from those who had heard the prosecutor's statements that day and lining up lawyers to represent him, should Loggins carry out his threat of pursuing a contempt action. In a move that garnered enormous respect from Townley and others, Cook's daughter Kristina Cook Connelly (now Graham) agreed to sign on as one of the lawyers willing to represent the defense attorney if a contempt action was actually brought, though it would mean standing up to her father as well as the judge. This kind of integrity eventually paid dividends, as she sits on the Superior Court judge's bench alongside then-prosecutor Ralph Van Pelt today. Van Pelt and other members of the district attorney's office were not keen on the idea of prosecuting the contempt, and shortly after this, the judge dropped the idea.

Having already been convicted once and sentenced to death, Tony West was more amenable to considering a plea than he originally had been. After much negotiating, Townley and the district attorney's office brokered a deal that would allow West to plead to the two murders and one armed robbery and receive life sentences rather than death. October 26, 1984, was the date set for the plea. The defendant panicked and balked at the last minute, however. Co-counsel Bobby Lee "Buzz" Cook Jr. was taxed with the unenviable chore of informing Judge Loggins that his client did not, in fact, wish to change his plea. Lomenick, who had been on the fence already about the plea as he was afraid of the political ramifications of allowing someone already sentenced to death to plead to life instead, announced vociferously that he was reinstating his request for the death penalty.

Red continued to waver about the best course of action to resolve the matter. His assistants, well aware of the anger of the citizens of the county over the cost of the wasted first trial, urged him to allow a plea to life imprisonment, if and when the defendant agreed to that. David L. Whitman, who had joined the office fresh out of law school after the trial in 1983 and who had worked on the appeal, assured the district attorney that the people of the county would certainly not be angry over such a plea. Around this same time, Whitman got his own taste of how Chattooga County's highly opinionated citizens could get riled up over a trial, particularly when the flames were fanned by the local media.

The district attorney's office had indicted a Trion Church of God of the Union Assembly minister and his wife for involuntary manslaughter because they had foregone medical care in favor of faith healing when their foster son developed appendicitis, and the boy subsequently died. The couple hired Bobby Lee Cook to represent them, and District Attorney Lomenick knew he was in trouble. Rather than try the case himself, he handed it off to

Whitman, his most inexperienced assistant. At trial, Cook persuaded Judge Loggins to direct a verdict against the state so that the case was thrown out without the defense ever having to present any evidence. The newspapers gleefully reported that, like Daniel being thrown to the lions, "Dancing Dave" Whitman had been thrown to the Great White Shark, Bobby Lee Cook. They went on to point out that Cook had chopped him into fishbait. The nickname "Fishbait" followed Whitman around the circuit for quite a while after that.

A motion was filed for a change of venue in the West case. Six witnesses testified that it was impossible to get an unbiased jury in Chattooga County. What was not brought out in testimony was the fear that another plea attempt, if brought before Judge Loggins again, would likely again fall apart. For that reason, both Townley and the office's most senior prosecutor, Roland Enloe, agreed that a change in venue was desirable. The motion was granted the day before Halloween 1984. While the wheels of justice turn slowly, eventually, the case was transferred to Polk County, where it was assigned to Superior Court Judge Dan Winn. At last, the case was out of Judge Loggins's hands. On March 19, 1985, Judge Winn accepted Tony West's guilty pleas and sentenced him to consecutive life sentences. Yet that was not the end of the legal troubles connected with Corpsewood.

Chapter 14

THE PROPERTY CASE

The two convicts found very little loot, but that did not mean there was nothing of value at the castle. On the contrary, Dr. Scudder had amassed renaissance furniture and art worth tens of thousands of dollars. Even items that normally had very little value could probably have been sold for significantly more as "souvenirs," although many local folks instead helped themselves to trophies free of charge. Rosebushes were dug up and replanted at the homes of curiosity seekers, small items not nailed down were taken—rumor has it the "Beware of the Thing" sign was stolen and sold on eBay for quite a bit. Many who acquired these prizes, however, came to regret them. Joey Odom's prized rosebushes did not bring the collectors the joy they had brought him, but rather, several of the usurpers swore that bad luck plagued them from the time they appropriated Corpsewood property. Gradually, the bushes and items began making their way back home, in hopes that the return would atone for the original theft.

The quantity of LSD found in the manor would have had a high street value, though the murderers failed to find it. The vials were stored in the Chattooga County Sheriff's Office's evidence room. However, more than one source has told me that a substantial amount of the LSD has disappeared from the vials, beginning shortly after the trial. Not only that, but an attorney in the area told me in confidence that his clients began reporting to him that there was some high-quality "windowpane" LSD that began hitting the streets not long after the trial concluded.

The castle would have had value beyond simply the structure because of the sheer notoriety of the place. Unfortunately, the main buildings of Corpsewood were destroyed by fire not long after the murders. The Chicken House, in fact, was burned to the ground on January 5, 1983, before the criminal case ever went to trial. The pleasure chamber was no more. Another arsonist torched the manor itself shortly after West's trial was over, in 1983. The persistent rumor has been that this was done by a group of religious fanatics in an attempt to exorcise the grounds of evil. (It was not, as some have alleged since the release of the Dove Broadcasting tape on YouTube, instigated by that documentary, however. While a portion was filmed while the home still stood, the film was not actually released until after the fires.) The majority of this most iconic reminder of the area's most famous Satanist and his partner was reduced to ashes and a pile of brick, although the well house, the building housing the chemical toilet and parts of the gazebo, foundation and a bit of wall still stand. Vandals continued to scour the scorched remains, however. A brick from Corpsewood became the new status symbol among those hungry for a remnant of the infamous castle. The structural remnants were reduced

The gazebo with its arched openings is one of the few structures that remains intact. *Amy Petulla.*

The remains of Corpsewood are gradually being swallowed up as nature reclaims its own. *Amy Petulla.*

more and more as the building blocks found their way into various homes in the area. Yet again, the looters began reporting "accidents," injuries and tragedies occurring close in time to their taking of a brick, and yet again, the bits of masonry were restored, with mumbled apologies "just in case," before the takers rapidly fled.

Fortunately for the heirs, they had removed most valuable items and had secured property insurance prior to the castle fire. The items were stored in an attorney's office. By the manner in which he had disinherited his heirs, Charles Scudder set up an epic fight. He cut them out of his will in favor of his life companion, Joseph Odom, but given their age difference, Scudder failed to contemplate the possibility that Joey might predecease him or die at the same time. Joey Odom did no such planning and instead died without a will. Thus, if Charlie died first, the estate passed to Joey, and as he died intestate and without children, it would be distributed to his siblings, Mary Fiumefreddo, Cora Mae Franklin and Catherine Funk. In that case, a group of women whom Charles Scudder barely knew would receive the sum total of his life's labors. If it was determined, however, that Odom died first, the estate would pass to Scudder's heirs at law—that is, his living children, Saul, Fenris and Gideon Scudder, whom he had disinherited. Which would he have chosen, had he considered the question: the children from whom he had been estranged for years, for whom he held enough ill feelings to not leave them a single cent, or people he had rarely seen? Most likely, given the choice, he would have elected a third option. Tracey Wilson claimed that the victims discussed opening a halfway house for prisoners or a Satanic temple of sorts. No evidence has turned up that Charles ever discussed such a temple, although some friends have said he occasionally mentioned a desire to help former inmates. While there is no indication that he ever took any steps toward building a halfway house, snubbing society with such a grand gesture would certainly have appealed to Scudder. But in this situation, those "what ifs" mattered not one whit. The law does not provide for a decedent's unwritten possible wishes to come into consideration. However, as a practical matter, it must have gone through the various judges' minds when pondering their decision. And a variety of judges it was, indeed.

Neither Joey Odom's sisters nor Charlie Scudder's kids lived in Georgia. Presumably, neither knew the attorneys in the circuit. Odom's family elected to go with local attorney Archibald Farrar, a sensible choice. Scudder's children, however, decided to pull out the big guns, and fortunately for them, there was a veritable cannon who made his home office right there in Summerville, Georgia.

Bobby Lee Cook has received so many honors and recognitions that setting them all out here would be unwieldy, so a small representative list will give a taste of his many achievements. He was the first recipient of the Georgia Bar Tradition of Excellence Award, gave the inaugural lecture at Georgia State Law School, received the Lifetime Achievement Award from the National Association of Criminal Defense Lawyers and, most recently, was inducted into the Trial Lawyers Hall of Fame. The distinction most recognizable by the general public, however, is not one granted by any organization of lawyers. It has been repeatedly stated that the southern lawyer television character "Matlock" was based on Bobby Lee Cook. While his style might sometimes be folksy when examining his own client, those who have been shredded by his razor-sharp tongue during cross-examination would probably take umbrage to any description implying he was easygoing. Some claim he can hypnotize the subjects of his cross-examination. Whether or not this is true, anyone watching him make a recalcitrant police officer dance to his tune on cross can easily see how this rumor came about.

Some people criticize criminal defense lawyers because, as those people put it, "They defend people they know are guilty!" As one of the preeminent criminal defense lawyers in the country, Cook has been the recipient of more than his share of that type of criticism. That does not hold him up for a second. According to Judge Loggins, Bobby Lee has said he would defend the devil himself if he could. It would not be the first time Satan had been called in to court; in 1971, Gerald Mayo attempted to sue "Satan and his Staff" in the U.S. District Court of the Western District of Pennsylvania, as "Satan has placed deliberate obstacles in his path and has caused plaintiff's downfall," thereby inflicting him with misery on numerous occasions. (That case was ultimately dismissed, as there were jurisdictional issues and a problem with the proper method to serve the defendant.) What such critics fail to understand, at least until such time as they might be wrongly accused, was succinctly summed up by Cook in the *ABA Journal* on March 2, 2009: "If you can railroad a bad man to prison, you can railroad a good man. That's why we should always vigorously fight for the constitutional rights of even those who are most despised in our communities." Civil litigants like the Scudders knew that when they wanted the most vigorous courtroom brawler, Bobby Lee Cook was their man.

The property case was heard originally before the criminal case went to trial, in front of Chattooga County Probate Court Judge Jon Payne on February 13, 1983. The hearing was closed to the public and press. Judge Payne heard evidence from crime lab personnel, GBI employees and Teresa Hudgins and Joey Wells, the eyewitnesses to the crime. Forensic experts were unable to determine which of the men died first. Hudgins's earlier statements had indicated that Odom was shot again with Scudder's revolver after Scudder was killed because he was showing some sign of life. After some instructive horse-shedding by the Scudders' legal counsel, however, her story at the probate hearing was that it was Scudder whom Kenneth Brock shot with the revolver. The physical evidence, though, showed that the only bullet shot from Scudder's gun was fired into Odom's rather than Scudder's skull. Judge Payne therefore ruled in favor of Joey Odom's sisters.

Cook immediately appealed the decision to Chattooga County Superior Court, where it would be heard by his friend the Honorable Joseph E. Loggins. Judge Loggins found that the Simultaneous Death Statute applied and granted summary judgment in favor of Cook and his client, ruling that they won as a matter of law without the necessity of a trial. Farrar appealed to the Georgia Supreme Court, which found that, although Teresa Hudgins had claimed in Probate Court that Odom's body had not moved from the time he was first shot, she also testified that his body was initially lying mostly in the kitchen and partly in the dining room, whereas he was completely in the dining room when she left (which was also the position indicated by the crime scene evidence). They also found that, despite his testimony in the hearing that Odom had not moved or made a sound once he was first shot and that it was Scudder who was shot last, Joey Wells had in his initial statements indicated that it was Odom who had begun moaning after the shooting of both men and it was Odom whom Brock shot with the revolver. The court ruled that this created a question of fact, which made the grant of summary judgment improper and reversed the trial court's order.

After the case was sent back to the Superior Court, the parties finally settled. Odom's relatives got $5,000, a stone cat, some pictures and a portrait of Joey, and Scudder's heirs got the remainder. The real estate was sold in 1985 to Bernard R. Shell. A 2007 deed purporting to be from him transferred it to an Alabama man named Osborne.*

---

* The only Bernard R. Shell turned up in a records search, however, died six years before that deed was signed. It continues to be privately owned by Osborne, not by the forestry service, as many believe. The tax value of the forty acres is currently listed at just over $30,000.

Chapter 15

The Haunting or Curse
of Corpsewood

Agnew Myers, an estate specialist, cleaned, authenticated and valued many pieces of personal property in the estate and even repaired some. The winged, horned creature holding a mirror, when cleaned up, turned out to be gold leaf. It was missing a portion of hand, so Myers recarved that part. The Mephistopheles statue was bronze with a porcelain patina and was the most valuable piece of the lot. Bobby Lee Cook kept it and the golden harp. The first day he took the statue home, his wife, June, broke her leg taking the garbage out. She banished it from her house, and it was thereafter kept at his office, until eventually, Cook got rid of both pieces. Cook's associate Albert Palmour got a small statue of Quasimodo that is still in his possession, and Agnew Myers got the grandfather clock (though it was no longer crowned with the skull).

As to Scudder's self-portrait, though for a short while Cook's relative Roger Williams kept the painting, none of these serious, highly educated attorneys and businessmen wanted to keep it because, though they did not share the belief with the general public, many of them felt it was cursed. Palmour kept it in a drawer for years. It is currently in the possession of the same private collector who acquired the Mephistopheles statue, a skull painting, the gargoyle over the entrance and the harp. Though it no longer has its intricately carved frame and it has acquired several nicks and scratches along the way, the painting remains as eerie as ever. Most of the rest of the property was sold at auction. George Coker purchased a number of smaller items, such as the bell, some devil's head candlesticks

The winged mirror, table and several carved figures are examples of the priceless four-hundred-year-old furniture that filled Corpsewood Manor. *Bobby Gilliland.*

and a number of books. Many of the pieces, including the Baphomet stained glass and the massive carved bed, were purchased by a notorious firearms dealer out of Atlanta.

The firearms dealer had recently married the girl who put together magazines in his guard shack, quickly put her on his company's board and, around the time of the Corpsewood murders, they founded a new company that operated originally out of Atlanta and later broke into subsidiaries that were housed primarily in Tennessee. They sold kits internationally that could be put together into unregistered submachine guns. ATF records showed that, though it was a tiny company, its guns showed up in an extraordinarily large number of trace requests for guns used in gun crime, including at least one school shooting. An ATF investigation indicated the guns were being sold to international gun dealers, drug smugglers and others involved in organized crime. One of the guns, which resembled the tommy guns of gangster days, was advertised as a way to do "spring cleaning." Eventually, both were charged with federal gun crimes (though they were later reduced to misdemeanors). The wife believed in the Corpsewood curse, and blaming those items rather than karma for the charges and their divorce, she blasted the Baphomet glass into a pile of sparkling rubble with a machine gun, gathered all the remaining Corpsewood relics together (including the renaissance bed) and made a bonfire in the front yard with them. It is unknown exactly which items perished in this fire, but several pieces have not been seen since. Likewise, most of George Coker's items disappeared, thought to have been disposed of by an evangelist relative who believed them to be evil.

For many years, "Zeke Woodall, Nudist," occupied the Corpsewood grounds. In fact, he paved the entire pond area with Cadillac floor mats so that he could run barefoot and roll around naked with no risk of any essential parts being cut by a sharp stone. But alas, he also eventually passed from this world. The remains of Corpsewood became a hangout for teens, Satanists, devil worshippers, curiosity seekers, paranormal investigators and those who come to pay their respects to Charles and Joey. So many have visited that a permanent campfire area was established and can usually be found full of discarded trash, including many beer cans and bottles. Should you choose to visit, as the saying goes, "Please take only photos and leave only footprints."

The rusted remains of the metal outer kitchen door still lie on the ground near the former back entrance where it used to hang. These days, it is marked with the word "Ababa." A Google search returned several spell casters in Addis Ababa, Ethiopia, advertising love charms and curses. A well-known travel website calls Ababa a magical portal, and even the comments on Internet stories on such unrelated topics as war in the region are full of plugs for these purveyors of the occult craft. Other signs that practitioners of the dark arts may have visited can also be found at Corpsewood. Some contend an altar has been built with the removed bricks that have poured back into the property. Others claim this was actually a part of a chimney from the Chicken House.

Many of those who gather there to this very day report hearing haunting harp music and growling dogs that cannot be seen in solid form, and they have related a variety of paranormal experiences. Often they talk about feeling watched, and the rumors of bad luck befalling those who remove anything from the area continue. One writer mentions a penny mysteriously appearing on a path where it had not been moments before, calling out its siren song to be picked up, which the man almost obeyed—until remembering the curse and withdrawing his outstretched hand as if bitten. There are even those who claim they have encountered some type of very large, strange creature on the property. Most, like the one who claimed he had encountered "Bigfoot" in a cellar during Charles and Joey's residence

The utility door, now crossed with careless disregard for the words they walk over by those who never sought permission to do so during life. *Amy Petulla.*

Chicken House chimney remains or altar built of bricks returned by thieves who believe they felt the place's curse? *Amy Petulla.*

there, had these encounters after a serious bout of drinking at the property. At least one such report I received, however, was from someone who was stone-cold sober, with a solid reputation in the community. The descriptions vary widely, and to date no photo or other documentation has been put forth to support these claims. A report whose details are more consistent comes from the few who claim to have seen an older, ragged-looking man appear, speak briefly and disappear before their eyes.

Two days after turning in my original manuscript, I had a remarkable experience. While getting the kinks borne of months at a computer worked out, I mentioned to the masseur that I had just finished a book about the murders of two gay men in Trion. He asked if they had occurred years ago. When I answered 1982, he told me about visiting the burned-out ruins of Corpsewood with friends on a dare. They had planned to stay longer, but it was cold (he acknowledged it may have been December, but he was not sure), and when they arrived, though there were no other cars there, they found two odd men sitting in lawn chairs in the middle of where the house had been. They were nice enough, though dressed a bit shabbily. The two men, who appeared perhaps in their forties, told them that they met there at that spot on that same day every year. They chatted for a while about the tragedy that had happened on that spot many years before. The two strangers appeared disturbed by a loud vehicle running up and down the road interrupting the peace and quiet, and when the young man and his friends returned from exploring the woods, the pair were gone. I asked what they looked like, and besides remarking on their age and dress, he said that one was solidly built and one was smaller. I asked if the larger one had dark hair and the smaller one light. He said yes. I had a printed copy of the manuscript with photos in my car, and when I was done, I fetched it and showed him the photo of Charlie. His jaw dropped, and he said that the blond man was identical to the photo, right down to his style of dress. Make of it what you will.

As the woods have reclaimed the area, the site of the former Satanists' residence has become harder and harder to find. A lengthy hike through woods sometimes guarded by rattlesnakes and often marked with dire warnings is required, even if you are able to locate the correct drive. Frequent visitors have helpfully marked the turnoff with a boulder inscribed with a cross and the initials "CW." If, however, you come with bad intent, you may find yourself thwarted. The Internet is full of blog posts from souvenir seekers unable to locate the castle in the country, even with careful directions. Dozens of others have reported that their cars crashed or simply died, refusing (as had the killers' own vehicle) to start if they removed something.

Right: This rock signals the pull-off where the path to Corpsewood begins. *Amy Petulla.*

Below: Many fallen trees guard the trail leading to the remains of the manor. Some have been marked with dire warnings. *Amy Petulla.*

The engine trouble reports began before the criminal investigation had even concluded or possibly even sooner. Charlie Moss of the crime lab was adamantly opposed to remaining on the property after dark but was forced to by the circumstances of the investigation. The next day, the transmission fell out of his car. The son of a friend of Scudder's, John Croy, reported that Scudder had a mischievous ability to cause car trouble during his lifetime and tells the tale of how, when visiting the professor to purchase some of his fine wine, his father refused Scudder's repeated attempts to persuade him to sell his car to him. Scudder laughingly told him that he would want to get rid of the car before long. Later that day, according to John, all four tires fell off the vehicle. An outlandish tale, perhaps—until you remember the police officer's account. Many people believe the victims' restless spirits remain at Corpsewood because their bodies rest there.

Chapter 16
THE BODIES

There are different reports about the disposition of the bodies of Charles Scudder and Joey Odom. Most people believe they were cremated and their ashes sprinkled at Corpsewood. Some maintain that Charles's ashes were taken back to Wisconsin by his sister and are buried where his memorial plaque lies at Forest Home Cemetery. Others say that the plot is empty, the plaque simply a symbol of remembrance. A different story was related by a police officer who wishes to remain anonymous, however.

Everyone agrees that there was excavation done at Corpsewood after the bodies were discovered there. The story given out to the general public and media was that the police suspected a secret underground lab there, and the excavation was done to try to uncover that. This tale makes the claim that the police simply "forgot" about the LSD highly suspicious. According to the officer who spoke in confidence, however, the underground lab was just a cover story. This witness states that Joey Odom had previously expressed his wish that, when he died, his body be buried in a specific part of the Corpsewood grounds and that the true purpose of the excavation was to dig Joey's grave without letting marauding members of the public know that his remains were there so that those remains would not be dug up, either by ghoulish souvenir seekers, by those seeking a source of magic or by zealous Christians seeking to destroy the temple of his body just as someone had destroyed their castle home, to rid the land of any remaining trace of the pair and their "heathen follies." Even their closest friends were not told, in order to protect the secret; they held a ceremony sprinkling what they believed to be his ashes at the property. If this burial in fact took place, Joey's sister did not share that information with her relatives who are still alive. To ensure that his body, if actually there, rests in peace, this book will not reveal the specific location on the property where the burial allegedly took place, but those who claim to feel the presence of the former housekeeper and companion may actually be closer to him than they realize when they visit.

Scudder, on the other hand, was unquestionably cremated. Sources say the cremation took place at the Tri-State Crematory. Like everything this case has touched, the crematory has since been painted with malfunction and scandal. It made national news in 2002, when more than three hundred uncremated bodies were discovered on the grounds, some lying out in the open, some mummified, some crammed into vaults packed to the brim with the remains of many and some reduced to a sort of malodorous biological soup, intermingling with the liquefied corpses of others such that the departed could not be differentiated in order to return the mortal remains to the grieving families. Ever since the discovery of that horrific landscape, people have been asking, "Why?" No one has been able to give an adequate explanation. Some think the answer starts with the arrival of the bullet-riddled bodies from Corpsewood Manor.

Tri-State Crematory was a new facility in 1982. It was established by Tommy Ray Marsh, a well-respected businessman in the area. Marsh did not simply work on the grounds of the crematory; he actually established his family's home on the grounds. Among those who moved into the home at the crematory was Ray's son, eight-year-old Ray Brent Marsh.

Ray Brent (also known simply as Ray to those who knew him or Brent in references to the criminal case) grew up on this land dedicated to the disposition of dead bodies. The acrid stench of burning flesh was his inheritance and birthright. He was living on the property when Charles Scudder and, according to most reports, Joey Odom arrived there almost as soon as he himself did.

The bodies of the two men were removed from Corpsewood in the back of a pickup truck that served as their hearse in the late afternoon hours of the day they were discovered. As they had lain in their own blood for several days before the discovery, they were already somewhat decayed. That, however, was not the reason the police were uncomfortable around them. These were almost all tough, seasoned officers. They had faced death before. It had been only a couple of months since the discovery in that county of the corpse of Janice Chatman, which was in far more deteriorated condition than these. And yet the men were all decidedly uncomfortable. No one wanted to remain in the vicinity of Scudder and Odom. When the bodies were at last taken away, the discomfort immediately lifted, as if a collective sigh had been heaved. According to Bobby Gilliland, the men glanced furtively at one another, and at last Billy Pledger, a state trooper, broke the silence: "I felt like something was watching us." This unleashed the floodgates. As it turned out, though none of them was by any stretch of the imagination superstitious, all of the men had felt an oppressive presence at the castle, one that went beyond the bounds of that evoked by dead bodies or even the unsettling contents of the home. As several of them expressed later to the media, they felt the presence of evil watching them—not that the victims were evil but that something malevolent was hanging about, observing the aftermath of the brutal murders. That ominous feeling, according to those willing to discuss it, departed immediately with the bodies.

The bodies were taken first to a local funeral home, where the autopsies were performed. They traveled in short order, however, to Tri-State Crematory, where young Brent Marsh resided. If these solemn, manly, experienced police officers were right, and there was indeed an evil presence that accompanied the bodies out of Corpsewood—thought by at least some of the officers to be the demon Charles Scudder had allegedly created—then a new home at an estate dedicated to dead bodies was a fitting destination for it. And this particular fiery depository was destined to acquire the notoriety that seemed to always accompany the remains of Corpsewood.

Brent Marsh grew up troubled by nightmares and insomnia. His mental and emotional condition deteriorated as his contact with the final destination of the corpses increased. His attorney, McCracken Poston, attributes this worsening state to a physical cause. Most corpses have at least a few dental fillings, and most of the older dental fillings contained mercury. Prolonged exposure to fumes containing mercury can cause madness. Indeed, the phrase "mad as a hatter" has its roots in mercury poisoning. Huguenot milliners created felt to shape into hats by matting together the fur of small animals and then using a smoothing agent that contained mercuric nitrate. Vapors released in the process contained free mercury, and if, as was often the case, they were working in a small, confined space, the hatters breathed the substance in. This resulted in mental confusion, emotional disturbance, neurological damage and muscular weakness. Men were more susceptible than women, according to Poston, because testosterone enhanced the effect. Similarly, because of a faulty ventilation system, both Brent Marsh and his father were constantly exposed to these vapors from the incineration of dental fillings containing mercury during the cremation process. The exposure led to organ damage in the elder

Marsh, but for Brent, the psychological effects were far worse. Just as with the milliners of old, Brent Marsh was eventually driven to madness. Whether this madness arose simply from the mercury or was exacerbated by the so-called curse of Corpsewood is for you, the reader, to decide.

In 1996, the multiple medical problems experienced by Tommy Marsh—illnesses caused by mercury exposure, according to Poston—caused the elder Marsh to turn over the reins of the business to his son. Although over the five years of his operation of the crematory the younger Marsh successfully cremated two-thirds of the bodies entrusted to him, at some point he stopped incinerating the remains, and 334 corpses were abandoned or stored in barns, vaults and vehicles on the sixteen-acre property. Though most people believe that the dust they receive after a loved one is cremated is the decedent's ashes, that is not actually the case. The temperatures required for cremation are so high that the ashes are consumed. Instead, the "cremains" given to grieving families are in fact the ground-up portions of bones that did not completely crumble to cinders. In this case, however, the contracting funeral homes were given ground-up cement instead.

It has been reported in some circles that this practice began because a part on the cremation oven broke. While it is true that there was a part broken on the ovens at the time the bodies were finally discovered—a part that could have been replaced at a relatively low cost—the fact of the matter was that when the bodies first began to be abandoned and discarded on the property, the oven was still in good working order. The cause of the nightmare Tri-State would eventually become was not a malfunctioning oven but the madness of the man who had grown from a small boy tormented by personal demons on this necropolis.

Though reports had been made to the Walker County Sheriff's Office of body parts around the crematory grounds in the fall of both 2000 and 2001, the police found nothing either time in their investigation of those reports. However, when authorities received a report that someone walking their dog had found a human bone on the property on Valentines Day 2002, their investigation the next day uncovered what would eventually total more than three hundred bodies on the grounds, bodies that had been accumulating there since 1996. What had changed in those few short months to render the field of cadavers suddenly visible to authorities? No one knows.

Chapter 17

Rest in Peace

Nowhere outside the fictional town of Castle Rock has such a plethora of aberrant crime flourished in such a small community. For fifteen years, however, Trion and its surrounds have again rested peacefully. There have been crimes, even murders, but they have been part of the landscape

Graffiti at Corpsewood. *Amy Petulla.*

of a small town rather than something out of a Hieronymus Bosch painting. When the virtual shroud that had concealed the hundreds of bodies at Tri-State was finally ripped off, the bodies were brought to light so that, at last, the dead could slumber. The healing of Northwest Georgia, which had suffered horror after horror, could begin. The curse of Corpsewood and its figurative demons seem to have been laid to rest, once and for all. Finally, the grounds and surrounds of Corpsewood Manor are at peace.

TIMELINE

1976: Howard Finster has a vision to create sacred art.

1976–77: Joey Odom and Charles Scudder move to Trion.

1982: The Marsh family moves to the Tri-State Crematory grounds.

1982: Scudder claims to create a demon.

1982: Finster buys World's Folk Art Church and converts it to look like a giant wedding cake.

Fall 1982: Judith Neelley and Alvin Neelley go on their murder spree.

December 1982: Scudder and Odom are murdered.

December 1982: Scudder and possibly Odom's bodies are delivered to Tri-State Crematory.

1996: Brent Marsh takes over operations at Tri-State and begins abandoning bodies on the grounds.

January 2000: Hayward Bissell murders and dismembers Patricia Booher.

October 2001: After a civilian complaint of bodies there, officers find nothing at Tri-State Crematory.

October 2001: Finster dies.

February 2002: More than three hundred bodies are found at Tri-State.

Bibliography

AboveTopSecret. "Corpsewood Manor: Would You Go There?/MKUltra." www.abovetopsecret.com/forum/thread551889/pg1.

Ancestry.com. Jessie Grimes family tree.

AP News Archive. "Legislator, Judge Among 11 Indicted in Drug, Money-Washing Case." November 15, 1985. www.apnewsarchive.com/1985/Legislator-Judge-Among-11-Indicted-In-Drug-Money-Washing-Case/id-c5ea7c7ce5a846eaf029e4fe5d85ec0a.

Arey, Norman. "Is Character Flaw Marsh's Undoing? Some Doubt Tragedy Involves a Crime (Tri-State Crematory)." *Atlanta Constitution*, April 7, 2002. www.freerepublic.com/focus/news/661187/posts.

Barclay, Delores. "Fourteen Women Now Sit on Death Row." *Chillicothe (MO) Constitution Tribune*, April 11, 1984.

Bonner, John. "Jury Acquits Powell." *Rome News-Tribune*, August 31, 1975, 1A.

Budd, James. *Murder at Corpsewood*. GA: Espy Publishing Company, 1983.

———. "What's Going On?" *Summerville News*, March 8, 1984, 4A.

Carson High School Yearbook, 1972.

Chattooga County Deed Records.

Chattooga Press. "Victim's Dad: Judith Neelley 'Killed' Again." June 1, 1996, 1.

The Conspiracy Theory Blogger. "From the Archives: A Look Back at Corpsewood." April 25, 2007. theconspiratorsnest.blogspot. com/2007/04/from-archives-look-back-at-corpsewood.html.

Cook, Thomas H. *Early Graves.* New York: Penguin Group, 1990.

"Corpsewood Manor: A New Perspective." www.facebook.com/ chattanoogaghosttours/app/410312912374011.

Cowboy21_357. "The Truth About Corpsewood Manor." April 23, 2009. thetruthaboutcorpsewoodmanor.blogspot.com/2009/04/truth-about-corpsewood-manor.html.

Curriden, Mark. "Bobby Lee Cook." *ABA Journal*, March 2, 2009.

Devier v. State, 250 Ga. 652 (300 SE2d 490) (GA 1983).

Estate of Charles Scudder. Chattooga County Probate Court, Georgia, 1983.

Explain Like I'm Five. "What Exactly Does LSD Do to Your Brain?" www.reddit.com/r/explainlikeimfive/comments/1xm490/eli5_what_exactly_does_lsd_do_to_your_brain.

Facebook. "Bourtai Hargrove." www.facebook.com/bourtaih.

———. "Corpsewood Manor—A Castle in the Woods." https://www. facebook.com/corpsewoodmemorial.

———. "Saul Scudder." https://www.facebook.com/search/ top/?q=saul%20scudder.

Find-a-Grave. "Dr. Charles Lee Scudder." www.findagrave.com/cgi-bin/ fg.cgi?page=gr&GRid=114724659.

———. "Joseph D 'Joey' Odom." www.findagrave.com/cgi-bin/fg.cgi?page=gr&GRid=114723296.

Fiumefreddo v. Scudder, 252 Ga 279 (GA 1984).

Gard, Richard, Jr. "Court Upholds Right to Counsel." *Fulton County (Atlanta, GA) Daily Report,* July 24, 1987, 1, 3.

Georgia House of Representatives. "A Resolution Commending Gary W. McConnell." House Resolution 756, 2011.

Georgia's Paranormal Places. "Corpsewood Manor." April 10, 2011. georgiasparanormalplaces.wordpress.com/tag/dr-charles-scudder.

Greenville Advocate. "Life Sentence Given NEELLEY by Butler County Jury." February 12, 1953.

Hernandez v. Texas, 347 U.S. 475, 74 S.Ct. 667, 98 L.Ed. 866 (1954).

Hunter, Marnie. "Howard Finster's 'Paradise': The South's Most Inspired Garden." CNN.com, 2014. www.cnn.com/2014/11/12/travel/paradise-garden-howard-finster.

Janesville Daily Gazette. November 17, 1967, 16. www.newspapers.com/newspage/10134079.

Johnson, Sheila. *Blood Highway.* AL: Pinnacle, 2008.

Komonews.com. "Man Wins Scratch Lottery Grand Prize…Again!" April 23, 2001. www.komonews.com/news/archive/4002986.html

Larson, Erik. "The Story of a Gun." *The Atlantic,* January 1993. www.theatlantic.com/magazine/archive/1993/01/the-story-of-a-gun/303531.

Lonely Planet. "Addis-Ababa." www.lonelyplanet.com/ethiopia/addis-ababa.

Lowrance v. State, 183 Ga. App. 421 (GA 1987).

Machetti v. Linahan, 679 F2d 236 (11th Cir. 1982).

Madison Wisconsin State Journal, September 28, 1949, and April 11, 1967.

May, Rachel. "You're Smiling in Corpsewood!" www.angelfire.com/corpsewoods/about.html.

Mckenna, Kristine. "The Rev. Howard Finster: How Great Thou Art?: From His Back-Yard Masterpiece to L.A. Galleries, the Georgia Painter Is Spreading the Good Word." *LA Times*, October 23, 1988.

Michigan Marriage Records, 1867–1952.

Mondschein, Ken. "The Society for Creative Anachronism." SCAToday. net, February 2, 2004. www.scatoday.net/node/1678.

Neelley v. State, 261 Ala 290, 293 (AL 1954).

1940 U.S. Federal Census records, Sixteenth Census of the United States

Noth, Pierre. "Judith Ann Neelley Needs to Leave Prison in a Casket." *Rome News-Tribune*, March 7, 1999, F-2.

OCGA § 15-12-40 (a) (1).

Pace, David. "Man May Use Drug Defense in Murder Trial." *Sumter Daily Item*, March 2, 1983, 4B.

Paradise Garden Self Guided Tour Booklet. N.p.: Paradise Garden Foundation, n.d.

People v. Welch, 131 Ill. App.2d 98 (IL 1971).

Perry, Tim. "Georgia Sheriffs Honor McConnell, Eyewitness to Slayings in Chattooga." *Rome News-Tribune*, July 15, 1983, A-3.

———. "Summerville Woman Says Romance Blossoms with Death Row Inmate." *Rome News-Tribune*, June 17, 1983, A-1.

———. "Witnesses Detail Victims' Hospitality Prior to Slayings at 'Corpsewood.'" *Rome News-Tribune*, January 27, 1983, A-3.

Purcell, Pam. "Court Overturns West's Conviction." *Chattooga Press*, January 20, 1988, 1.

r/LSD. "What Are Hallucinations from LSD Like?" www.reddit.com/r/LSD/ comments/umeeo/what_are_hallucinations_from_lsd_like_ive_never.

Robinson, B.A. "'McMartin' Ritual Abuse Cases in Manhattan Beach, California." ReligiousTolerance.Org. October 29, 2005. www.religioustolerance.org/ra_mcmar.htm.

Rome News-Tribune. "Couple's Trial on Foster-Son's Death Expected This Week." February 26, 1984, 2A.

———. "Samuel Tony West Rejects Plea to Avoid Death Row." October 26, 1984, A-1.

Satanic Stalker. "Anno Satanas." January 26, 2009. community.beliefnet.com/go/thread/view/43861/13787171/?liveView=1.

Scott, John. *Corpsewood: The Remains.* N.p.: Amazon, 2014.

Scudder, Charles L. "A Castle in the Country." *Mother Earth News*, March/April 1981.

———. "A Study on the Activity, Ethology and Psychology of Fluorescent Plastic Cubes." *Worm Runner's Digest* 15, no. 1 (December 1973): 122–26.

State v. Judith Neelley file. Lookout Mountain Judicial Circuit District Attorney's Office (GA 1983).

State v. Tony West exhibit file, Chattooga County Superior Court (GA 1983).

State v. Tony West trial transcript, Chattooga County Superior Court (GA 1983).

A sympathetic reprobate. "A Satanist's Guide to William Blake." www.churchofsatan.com/introduction-to-william-blake.php.

Syrakousina, Anna Dokeianina. "Religion and the SCA: An Opinion." Anachronistic and Impulsive. March 5, 2014. annasrome.com/2014/03/05/religion-and-the-sca-an-opinion.

Taksier, Henry. "Welcome to the Current Middle Ages." *Satellite Magazine*, March 2010, reprinted at gracestainback.wordpress.com/2010/04/22/welcome-to-the-current-middle-ages.

Tegegne, Prof. Muse. "Eritrea Warns of Ethiopia War 'Sabre-Rattling.'" Yahoo News, September 8, 2015. www.eritrea-beligerance.com/2015/09/eritrea-warns-of-ethiopia-war-sabre.html.

Thompson, Joanne. *Corpsewood*. Directed and performed by Joanne Thompson. 1984. Greenville, SC: WGGS Dove Broadcasting. Documentary.

tunnelrat. "A Little Timeline." Uzitalk.com MAC forum, May 16, 2008. www.uzitalk.com/forums/showthread.php?35853-MAC-History-Lesson-Requested.

United States ex rel. Gerald Mayo v. Satan and His Staff, 54 F.R.D. 282 (1971).

The Vaults of Erowid. "LSD-25." www.erowid.org/chemicals/lsd/lsd.shtml.

Waters, Robert. "'An Extraordinarily Gruesome Case,' or Why Everyone Needs a Gun." www.conservativebookstore.com/bestdefense/messages/25.html.

West, Shannon, Susan E. Scott and Teresa Hudgins. *Corpsewood: The Eyewitness Account*. N.p.: Dark Hollows Press, 2015.

West v. State, 252 Ga. 156, 313 S.E.2d 67 (GA 1984).

Wikipedia. "The Blizzard of 1977." en.wikipedia.org/wiki/Blizzard_of_1977.

Yanez, Luisa. "Jan. 19, 1977: The Day It Snowed in Miami." *Miami Herald*, January 19, 2007. www.miamiherald.com/latest-news/article1931272.html.

YouTube. "Part 1 Catoosa County 'Meet the Candidates' Rally, June 23, 1988." www.youtube.com/watch?v=UGeoleWWN64.

Index

About the Author

Amy Petulla is familiar with the Corpsewood murder case from both legal and paranormal standpoints. She began practicing law in 1986, when David "Red" Lomenick hired her as an assistant district attorney. The Tony West murders were a topic of local interest from the time she arrived. Amy was a trial attorney for twenty years and now mediates and writes. She is the co-author of *Haunted Chattanooga* and the owner of Chattanooga Ghost Tours, Inc. Amy has a BA in psychology from Emory University and a JD from the University of Georgia.

By Bob Edens.